Winning Together

UX research, the key to comprehending users' behaviors, motivations, and preferences for developing delightful experiences, thrives on effective teamwork and collaboration. This comprehensive guide brings together the expertise and insights from seasoned researchers, cross-functional partners, and product leaders in order to transform how you collaborate and unlock the true potential of UX research.

Key Features:

- Includes a comprehensive selection of ready-to-use templates
- Incorporates insights and advice from cross-functional stakeholders
- Offers a wide range of strategies tailored to various expertise levels, catering to both novice and advanced practitioners
- Presents universally applicable methodologies and insights, equipping a diverse range of researchers, including consultants, vendors, and in-house professionals.

From experienced professionals to those starting out, and freelancers to in-house researchers, this comprehensive guide offers practical strategies to navigate the pitfalls of UX research, enhancing collaboration and, ultimately, driving success.

Winning Together
A UX Researcher's Guide to Building Strong Cross-Functional Relationships

Sonal Srivastava

CRC Press
Taylor & Francis Group
Boca Raton London New York

CRC Press is an imprint of the
Taylor & Francis Group, an **informa** business

First edition published 2024
by CRC Press
2385 NW Executive Center Drive, Suite 320, Boca Raton FL 33431

and by CRC Press
4 Park Square, Milton Park, Abingdon, Oxon, OX14 4RN

CRC Press is an imprint of Taylor & Francis Group, LLC

© 2024 Sonal Srivastava

ISBN: 978-1-032-48836-3 (hbk)
ISBN: 978-1-032-48835-6 (pbk)
ISBN: 978-1-003-39103-6 (ebk)

DOI: 10.1201/9781003391036

Typeset in Palatino
by Apex CoVantage, LLC

To my incredible mother,

This book is a testament to your tireless efforts in raising me and the invaluable

lesson that you taught me—that there are no limits to what I can achieve.

Contents

About the Author

Sonal Srivastava is a seasoned UX researcher with over 15 years of experience working across diverse industries, including Amazon, Meta, Instacart, and Blizzard. Based in Seattle, Sonal holds a double Master's degree in Social Psychology from the University of Delhi and Human-Centered Design from the University of Washington, Seattle. Her passion lies in guiding companies in harnessing the full potential of user research for creating delightful products as well as developing the next generation of UX researchers.

Her global experience—having lived and worked across continents from India and Ghana to China and the USA—has cultivated a deep understanding of cultural nuances. This, combined with her vast experience spanning from dynamic startups to established corporate giants, has honed her skills in effective stakeholder management and crafting bespoke UX research strategies.

When she's not conducting research or writing, Sonal can be found exploring new places with her husband and two adventurous daughters. She has a passion for experimenting with new recipes in the kitchen, is an ardent wildlife enthusiast, and actively works toward advocating for wildlife conservation.

Additional Contributors

Saeideh Bakhshi—Saeideh Bakhshi is a data-driven insight leader with over 15 years of experience in research in academia and industry. She holds a Ph.D. degree from Georgia Tech and has worked with some of the world's largest tech companies, such as Yahoo, Facebook, and Google. *www.linkedin.com/in/saeideh-bakhshi-68a3676/*

Kyle Brady—Kyle Brady is a research lead who has been conducting human-centered research for more than a decade, working in the fields of cognitive psychology, HCI, and currently user experience. *www.linkedin.com/in/kylejamesbrady/*

Todd Carmody—Todd Carmody is a strategy and innovation consultant based in New York and Berlin. He has held postdoctoral fellowships at Harvard, UC Berkeley, and the Freie Universität Berlin and is the author of *Work Requirements* (Duke University Press, 2022). *www.linkedin.com/in/toddcarmody/*

Lillian Chen—Lillian Chen is a product designer from the Bay Area and has worked at various tech companies such as Meta and Omada Health. She holds a master's degree in media and communications from the London School of Economics and Political Science. www.linkedin.com/in/chenlilliant/

Theo Folinas—Theo Folinas, Staff Product Designer at Thrive Market, brings a wealth of experience from previous roles at Instacart, Thumbtack, and more. *www.linkedin.com/in/theofolinas/*

Linnea Hagen—Linnea Hagen is a Sr. UX research manager based in Seattle. She has worked for companies such as Amazon, Microsoft, and Tobii Eye Tracking and is passionate about building impactful, curious, and skilled research teams. *www.linkedin.com/in/linnea-hagen-4b551b13/*

Ali Horowitz—Ali Horowitz is a content designer at Meta with over seven years of experience in tech, including as a UX researcher. She has a Ph.D. degree in psychology from Stanford University. *www.linkedin.com/in/alihorowitz/*

Kamyar Keshmiri—Kamyar Keshmiri, VP, Global Head of Design at Amazon Prime Video, merges storytelling and innovation to launch beautiful products that humanize technology and bring shape to the future. With extensive experience at Warner Bros and IDEO, he is an accomplished design leader that strives to scale impactful teams, deriving strategic advantage through design. *www.linkedin.com/in/kamyarkeshmiri/*

Stephanie Kim—Stephanie Kim is a UX researcher, passionate about creating accessible, community-driven experiences. She holds a bachelor's degree in Cognitive Science from UC San Diego and has worked across various domains such as health design (UCSD Design Lab) and grocery tech (Instacart). *www.linkedin.com/in/stephaniehjkim/*

Anubhav Kushwaha—Anubhav Kushwaha is a director of Engineering at DoorDash, with a career spanning companies such as Amazon, Microsoft, and Martjack. He holds a BE from IIIT Calcutta. *www.linkedin.com/in/anubhavkushwaha/*

Anne Mamaghani—Anne Mamaghani is a seasoned UX leader with extensive experience, including leadership roles at Yahoo!, eBay, and Meta. Anne holds an M.S. in human factors in Information Design and a B.A. in journalism and women's studies. As Founder + CEO of Wisdom Driven UX, she helps companies increase revenue, reduce operational costs, and boost key metrics through a strategic understanding of their customers. You can find her at *www.wisdomdrivenux.com* and *www.linkedin.com/in/annemamaghani/*

Ilana Meir—Ilana Meir is a staff conversation designer at Meta's Reality Labs. She specializes in Augmented Reality environments and applying AI to improve conversational experiences. She holds an M.A. in integrated marketing communications from Northwestern University and has contributed to several books. *www.linkedin.com/in/seamstressofstories*

Kevin Mendoza—Kevin Mendoza is a content designer in San Francisco. He has worked for tech companies—large and small—in and around the Bay Area. *www.linkedin.com/in/kevinmendozasf/*

Omer Muzaffar—Omer Muzaffar is a product management leader in the Greater Seattle area. He has over ten years of experience working on a wide portfolio of consumer technology products at Meta Reality Labs and Amazon. *www.linkedin.com/in/omermuzaffar/*

Sean Ryan—Sean Ryan is currently a UXR lead at Google. He has conducted qualitative research for close to 20 years in the technology and consumer products realm. He has a background in anthropology and specializes in ethnographic and video storytelling approaches. *www.linkedin.com/in/sean-ryan-5143691/*

Tom Satwicz—Tom Satwicz is a vice president of Research at Blink UX and a graduate of the Ph.D. program in learning sciences at the University of Washington. He loves helping teams gain empathy for anyone that uses their product or service. *www.linkedin.com/in/tsatwicz/*

Aditya Sharma—Aditya Sharma is a senior design manager at Microsoft with 14 years of design experience, specializing in games. Holding a master's degree in human-computer interaction from Carnegie Mellon, he has honed his skills at renowned companies like EA, Caradigm, and GE, delivering innovative and immersive gaming experiences. *www.linkedin.com/in/adityakrsharma/*

Sarah Simpson—Sarah Simpson is a seasoned product designer with a decade of experience. She currently works at Meta, where she focuses on virtual reality design. Her philosophy centers on creating impactful, immersive experiences that are meaningful and cohesive for users. Sarah holds a Bachelor of Fine Arts degree from Virginia Tech. *www.linkedin.com/in/sarahtannerdesigns/*

Wyatt Starosta—Wyatt Starosta, over the past 20 years, has led design research and strategy programs that have helped companies get to the essence of the consumer experience. These programs have identified new product and service opportunities for companies, including Microsoft, Procter & Gamble, Nike, Samsung, and Chrysler. *www.linkedin.com/in/wyattstarosta*

Amelie Werner—Amelie Werner, global head of design operations, UX Research & Global Commerce Design at Amazon Prime Video, has left her mark at both Amazon and Microsoft. She combines her expertise to drive impactful user experiences and operational excellence in the streaming industry. *www.linkedin.com/in/ameliewerner/*

1

Introduction

DOI: 10.1201/9781003391036-1

The *"Why"* Behind the Book

As UX researchers, you might often face many challenges, including but not limited to the following:

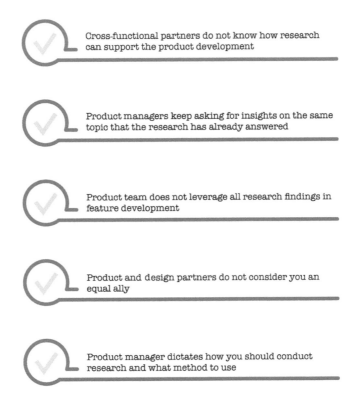

Cross-functional partners do not know how research can support the product development

Product managers keep asking for insights on the same topic that the research has already answered

Product team does not leverage all research findings in feature development

Product and design partners do not consider you an equal ally

Product manager dictates how you should conduct research and what method to use

As a user experience researcher for over a decade, I have faced countless challenges when collaborating with my cross-functional partners. It was not always easy to establish myself as a thought partner to the team or to persuade them to effectively apply research findings, let alone to make a significant impact. However, with the invaluable insights gained from past experiences, I now have a more informed perspective, enabling me to make better decisions and drive change.

I have worked in diverse settings, ranging from a six-person start-up, where I found myself having to justify my role to the team, to a nonprofit organization, where I had to navigate stakeholders who were not well-versed in the tech world. I have worked both as a consultant and as an in-house researcher, which has forced me to adapt to different organizational cultures, expectations, and team dynamics. My work as a pathfinding researcher for one company lasted an entire year, giving me ample time to dive deep into the project and build meaningful relationships with my team. In contrast, the fast-paced environment at a social media company meant that my projects lasted anywhere from two weeks to two months, keeping me on my toes and demanding quick results.

Through all these varied experiences, one core element remained consistent—the importance of influencing cross-functional partners to deliver impact. However, achieving this required sparking empathy and working hand in hand with them, *and it was not easy*. Over the years, I have seen many failures, and each one of them gave me lessons to get better at them. My learnings came not only from managers, fellow researchers, and mentors but also significantly from the cross-functional partners themselves.

In this book, I have curated a wealth of actionable ideas, ready-to-use templates, proven strategies, and compelling stories and advice that extend beyond my own journey and incorporate the collective wisdom of successful researchers, cross-functional partners, and product leaders. By tapping into this diverse wealth of knowledge, my intention is to equip you with the tools and guidance needed to navigate the challenges of UX research, avoid common pitfalls, and gain the confidence to excel in your role.

Whether you're a seasoned veteran in the field or just starting out, this book has advice for everyone. It caters to freelancers, external consultants, and in-house researchers, offering numerous strategies to build strong relationships with cross-functional partners, establish a solid foundation, and deliver impactful results.

In this book, I share common mistakes UX researchers tend to make throughout their careers. Then we explore practical strategies that can be implemented on a day-to-day basis to overcome those challenges. Additionally, we also talk about long-term approaches to becoming successful product partners.

If you ever find yourself thinking that your cross-functional partners are not leveraging your research or you wish for greater collaboration, refer to this book and identify which strategies you have yet to try and try to implement them.

DISCLAIMER
I do want to add a *Disclaimer* here—it's important to note that not all strategies mentioned may be universally applicable. Organizational cultures, processes, team sizes, and resources vary significantly across different organizations. Furthermore, the level of support for UX research can also vary greatly among organizations. It is also essential to recognize that distinctions may exist between team members who are embedded within the organization and those who work as external consultants.

Therefore, do your due diligence to determine which strategies are most suitable for your particular situation. By being discerning and thoughtful in your approach, you can determine which strategies are most likely to yield success and positively impact your work.

2

Who Are (Your) Cross-Functional Partners and Why Is Their Buy-In Important?

DOI: 10.1201/9781003391036-2

Who are cross-functional partners?

For a UX researcher, cross-functional (XFN) partners are your work colleagues with different functional expertise who support the same product as you and, ideally, should leverage the findings from your research to inform strategic product decisions. This group may include peers such as program managers, product managers, designers, design program managers, data analysts, and software engineers, as well as their respective managers and the leadership team.

Are you more accustomed to using the term stakeholder instead?

"Stakeholder" is a broader term that encompasses anyone with a stake or an interest in the product or service being developed and also includes team members such as customers, other user experience researchers, market researchers, design operations, and legal counterparts. While cross-functional partners are a type of stakeholder, not all stakeholders are necessarily cross-functional partners.

The techniques discussed in this book are applicable to all stakeholders. However, it places particular emphasis on strategies tailored explicitly for cross-functional partners, especially those who support diverse product functions.

You must be thinking, why do you need to make extra efforts to influence your cross-functional partners if they are working on the same product as you and you are all working toward the success of the same product?

As researchers, we are passionate about understanding our users and building user-centric products, but we often forget to "make the case" with our cross-functional partners. When talking to the users, some insights are more obvious to us, but that does not mean it's obvious to our product, design, and software engineering counterparts. Half of a user researcher's job is to do powerful research, but the other half is getting cross-functional partners to care about the research and the insights.

How we create, measure, and communicate our impact is essential to up-level our function, and I am excited to go deeper into how researchers can do these more effectively.

Before going forward and learning about the strategies to influence your cross-functional partners, we need to outline who your cross-functional partners are. This list could vary depending on your organization, whether you support the team as an embedded researcher versus an external consultant, and the staffing on the particular product.

A common misconception is that researchers only support designers, as research is essentially seen as the support system that helps evaluate UX designs. Research and design indeed partner well, as they should, but an effective researcher and a thought leader should partner with cross-functional partners from all disciplines.

Prototyping   **Development**   **Testing**

In my career spanning over a decade, I have partnered closely with product managers, program managers, data scientists, designers, content designers, business development managers, and software engineers at all levels.

At this point, you must be asking yourself, "Do the same approach work across cross-functional partners from all disciplines?" Essentially yes. The fundamentals of collaboration remain the same. However, cross-functional partners from different disciplines benefit differently from research.

Researchers should work closely with **product managers** to support the product strategy by sharing research findings and emphasizing storytelling and trade-offs with them.

When collaborating with **software engineers**, I have discovered that they place significant emphasis on interaction design and value any user insights available to them. In addition, presenting edge cases is also essential in assisting them.

ⓘ SNEAK PEEK INTO DIFFERENT CROSS-FUNCTIONAL PARTNERS

Product manager: A product manager is responsible for the overall strategy, planning, and development of a product or products within a company. They ensure that the product meets customer needs while overseeing the product through its entire lifecycle.

Data scientist/data analyst: Data scientists specialize in collecting, processing, and analyzing large volumes of data to derive insights and make informed business decisions.

Designer: Designers focus on the interaction between real human users (like you and me) and everyday products and services, such as websites, apps, and even coffee machines. It's a highly varied discipline, including voice interface designers, industrial designers, visual designers, UX designers, graphic designers, etc.

Software engineer/developer: Computer or software engineer responsibilities include designing, testing, and inspecting all software used within an organization's computer system.

Content strategist/content designer: A content strategist is responsible for creating content in a user-friendly language needed for digital product experiences.

With **data scientists** partner closely to form a holistic view of data. They have access to user data and trends but often need more justifications behind the patterns they see. Research helps in closing that gap. I always aim to publish joint reports summarizing data from both data science and research. This provides leadership and other cross-functional partners with one source of truth and aids in decision-making.

To drive impact, researchers need to collaborate effectively and efficiently with all the product functions.

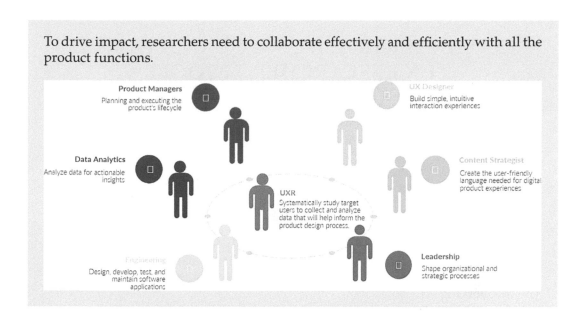

Next are **UX designers**—Research supports the product through the design development phase by conducting concept testing and usability studies. However, it is also critical for researchers to evangelize the value of foundational research and how it helps ground design decisions through a clear understanding of user needs.

I collaborate with **content designers**, also referred to as content strategists or UX writers, to assess content in the context of product experiences and how it resonates with users.

Last but not least is the **leadership**—Cross-functional partners that are not involved in day-to-day research but need research data for decision-making. For leadership, I focus on the summary or high-level takeaways of my research and the actionable recommendations the research proposes.

SAEIDEH BAKHSHI, SR. QUANTITATIVE UX RESEARCHER, GOOGLE

As a UX researcher, you will likely work closely with a variety of cross-functional partners, including product managers, designers, engineers, and data analysts. Collaboration between these teams is essential to ensure the user experience is optimized and business goals are met.

Here, I want to draw on some of my experiences working with cross-functional partners as a *quantitative UX researcher*.

IDENTIFYING KEY PARTNERS

It's important to identify which cross-functional partners are most critical to your work. This will vary depending on your specific role and the nature of the project you are working on.

Quantitative (quant) UX researchers, given the focus on quantitative methodologies like data analysis with logs or running surveys, are more likely to work closely with engineers, product managers, and data analysts, especially if they are working on internal metrics or product surveys.

In some cases and for some projects, quantitative UX researchers work closely with marketing as well; think of examples like segmenting user audiences and understanding various user needs and preferences.

Occasionally, depending on the project, quant UX researchers may also need close collaboration with designers. Examples of these projects where I have closely collaborated with designers are evaluating new concepts at scale, creating a gating mechanism for product launches and evaluating user experiences before launch by measuring the success of user journeys. Insights from research help designers address key users' pain points and design for quantitatively validated user preferences. This collaboration ensures that the final design is practical and functional for a broader set of users.

I've also enjoyed collaborating with designers in putting together visually aesthetic and more compelling presentations that summarize quantitative insights (that sometimes could be dry) with compelling visuals.

It's worth noting that the role of a quant UX researcher can vary widely depending on the organization and even the team that they are working with. Understanding where your role fits within the broader organization can help you identify which partners are most critical to your success.

3

Mistakes That UX Researchers Make With Cross-Functional Partnerships

DOI: 10.1201/9781003391036-3

Many of us would jump at the chance to rectify mistakes made during the first few years of our careers if given the opportunity for a do-over. Personally, I know I would.

Over the past ten years, I have gained a wealth of knowledge and experience that I wish I had possessed earlier in my career. Looking back, I realize the value of learning from mistakes and becoming wiser as a result.

In this chapter, I will highlight some of the common mistakes I made or saw other researchers make and the impact they had. In the subsequent chapters, I will provide you with actionable strategies and techniques to prevent these mistakes from happening or mitigate their effects.

Mistake 1—Underestimating Your Potential as a Strategic Collaborator

UX research helps teams build a deep understanding of people and insights that can shape the future. It can and should play an integral role in determining product strategy. However, researchers often undervalue or underestimate their role in product development and limit themselves to only executing projects given to them by product partners. This becomes problematic when cross-functional partners are not aware of the tools their research team has at their disposal, leading to underutilization of research.

Researchers are often hesitant to proactively suggest research for fear of having their ideas fall flat. Sometimes, they are unsure if product and design partners would care for the suggestion. At other times they do not think of research as having the same seat at the table as product and design counterparts.

To be an effective researcher, we need to work with cross-functional partners to answer the team's biggest questions about user behavior and user needs. Both the product lead and the UX researcher share the responsibility for achieving success in this endeavor. It is not only crucial for researchers to take the initiative and identify potential research areas that could provide valuable user insights, but they also need to partner with the product team at every stage of the product cycle to aid in decision-making.

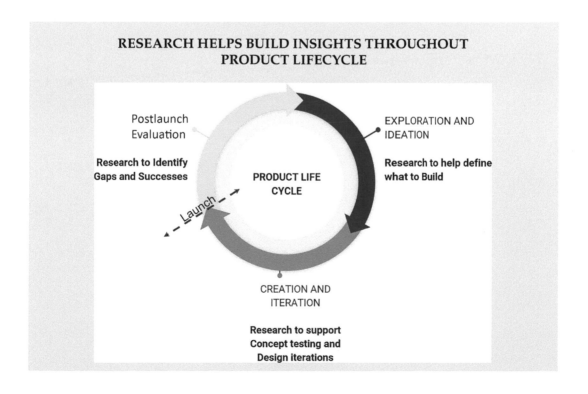

Do not limit your role to what has been set as an expectation.

Take the opportunity to guide your cross-functional partners on how they can leverage you and your expertise to glean into user pain points, needs, and behaviors and educate them on what a successful partnership looks like for a successful product launch.

Whenever I find myself hesitant to propose research or need to convince my cross-functional partners about the value of research, I turn to a story that I find to be an excellent resource to highlight the significance of research to non-research stakeholders.

IDEO, a design firm, faced the challenge of creating a new children's toothbrush for Oral-B. Despite initial skepticism, IDEO insisted on conducting field research and made a crucial observation: children hold toothbrushes differently than adults due to their limited dexterity. Armed with this insight, IDEO designed a big, fat, squishy toothbrush tailored to children's needs. The result was a best-selling product for Oral-B and prompted other toothbrush manufacturers to redesign their offerings.

This example demonstrates the power and credibility that come with conducting research that uncovers significant findings and drives success in the market.

ADITYA SHARMA, SR. DESIGN MANAGER, MICROSOFT

Over the past decade, I have worked on a broad spectrum of products, from enterprise healthcare products to gaming. In my experience, an essential ingredient of a successful product team is always a well-staffed UX research team. Taking an idea to a successful product requires a thorough understanding of customer problems. In today's SAS-driven world, research is critical in articulating customer pain points and helping product teams understand how and when these impact OKRs (*objectives and key results*).

A few years ago, when I was working at Xbox, Game Pass was a new and untested idea, and research played a major role in making it a success. The research team helped define user segments and tracked feedback that had the highest impact on our OKRs, giving the Design and Product teams the ability to rapidly iterate, test, and ship improvements. Research insights also helped inform what type of games we should add next. One of the metrics that users brought up was time to play, which can be significant in the case of AAA games since downloads are often north of 50–60 GB. Based on this insight, the team went after games with smaller install sizes. We noticed an improvement in the number of games the average Game Pass user was playing every month as the catalog expanded to include games that were fun to play and could be downloaded in minutes instead of hours. It also gave gamers something to play while waiting to download the latest AAA title to be added to Game Pass.

Without the involvement of research from the get-go and their proactive efforts to determine which research would be most beneficial and when, it would have been impossible for the product team to launch successful user-centered solutions. The research helped the team at every stage of the product life cycle:

1. Understanding the market landscape and user pain points during the creative phase
2. Validating assumptions and designs during the iterative phase
3. Tracking OKRs and feeding the product quality pipeline during the reactive/postlaunch phase

Research presented data that challenged our biases and encouraged healthy conversations between product managers, design, and developers that drove the product forward. It gave the team the ability to make conscious decisions on how they want to balance user and business needs and understand the consequences of those decisions.

Mistake 2—Not Owning Your Expertise

Are you guilty of asking your cross-functional partners questions about methodology or sample size, or have you observed other researchers posing questions to cross-functional partners such as:

> *"How many participants should I recruit for this upcoming study?"*
>   Or
>   *"Should we do card sort or conduct unmoderated interviews?"*

While the effort to appear as collaborative partners and establish relationships is admirable, it's important to remember that you are the expert and should take ownership of your craft. Collaboration does not mean that we forget to put on our "expert hat" and strut our stuff!

It is similar to your visual design partner asking you, "What should be the contrast ratio for text and background?"

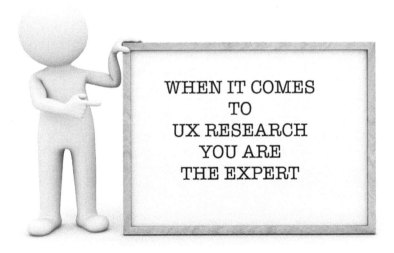

When we put together a research plan to execute a study, as experts in the field, it is our responsibility to assess all relevant methodologies for the research question, weigh the benefits and drawbacks of each, and then work collaboratively to determine the most suitable approach as a team. We need to lead the task of creating the interview guide and moderate sessions that best suit the objective.

Likewise, when codesigning the screener survey and the interview guide with the entire team, it is important to take the lead and ensure that all members are aligned with the research technique.

We may seek guidance from fellow researchers and collaborate with product team partners, but we need to remember that technical expertise is beyond the scope of our cross-functional partners' competency.

This is not to say that you should be dismissive of ideas or suggestions from your cross-functional partners; instead, you should take these moments to explain why you are recommending a certain methodology over others. We want to nurture an environment where everyone feels comfortable sharing their ideas, but at the same time, you want to establish yourself as the expert when it comes to UX research.

To summarize, you are the expert in research techniques; your cross-functional partners are not. Own your expertise! Be the leader and ensure all research protocols and techniques are rightly followed, even when co-planning with others on the team. And do not put the onus on cross-functional partners to detail the steps.

Cheatsheet: Knowing When to Collaborate and When to Assert Your Expertise

	Assert Your Expertise and Share For Feedback	Join Forces and co-develop
Objective of Study	✓	✓
Research Questions	✓	
Hypothesis	✓	✓
Reviewing Past Literature	✓	
Methodology	✓	
Study Timeline	✓	✓
Recruitment Criteria	✓	✓
Interview Script	✓	
Survey Responses	✓	✓ (For nominal questions)
Sample Size	✓	
Session Moderation	✓	
Analyses of Data	✓	✓
Report Writinga	✓	
Presentation of findings	✓	

WYATT STAROSTA, DIRECTOR, UX RESEARCH

The fine balance of asserting expertise and collaborating is not an easy one!

Our team of researchers was working with a new product manager (PM); he was a senior PM with several years of experience and was responsible for tapping into a new set of customers that would potentially unlock a new stream of revenue. The mandate from his director was to *gain a deep understanding of this new customer type so that they could develop the right set of features and functionality.*

We kicked off the project on a Monday with an hour-long meeting with the lead researcher, myself, two designers, and the PM. We discussed the goals of the project and the expected outcomes. We DID NOT discuss methodology because, well, that is the job of the research team to craft! We learned later this was one of those rare circumstances where it would have been helpful to touch on methodology as it would have illuminated the PM's discomfort with qualitative (qual) methods and, ultimately, what type of data would get him the most traction.

By the end of the meeting, the researcher and I walked away with a rough sketch of the project brief and a false sense of satisfaction that our PM partners were starting to understand that deep customer research would help them move more quickly and with greater confidence. It was that word "deep" that got us into trouble. During the kick-off, our PM used that word repeatedly, but his meaning was different than ours—and this would come to a head on the following Wednesday when we reviewed our research plan with him. We all came to the meeting excited to build off the energy from the previous Monday, but I could tell by the blank expression on his face that he was getting very uncomfortable with one aspect: small sample, qualitative interviews. While the lead researcher and I felt this was the best way to get deep insights about the customer, our PM was wholly unfamiliar with qualitative approaches, and he pushed for statistical significance and data that was "reliable." He wanted a large sample size; otherwise, he couldn't make decisions confidently. After explaining the trade-offs of depth for breadth in a quant versus qual approach, we learned that our PM wasn't really looking to understand his customers' goals, needs, mindsets, and motivations (which was our understanding of the meaning of 'deep'); what he really needed was market sizing data that could help him understand basic characteristics of his customers.

This was a valuable teaching moment for me, as it emphasized the importance of sharing the initial methodology and its benefits early in the research process. Although, as a researcher, it is my responsibility to determine the most appropriate methodology, sharing it early can facilitate early buy-in and alignment among stakeholders while reducing the likelihood of unexpected outcomes in the end.

Mistake 3—Not Involving Cross-Functional Partners at the Right Time

Have you ever been in a situation where your PM taps on your shoulder when you are actively moderating sessions (or right before) and asks, "Can you add these new questions to the interview script?" or raises concerns as to why you did not include a different sample when you present survey results?

This happens mostly when cross-functional partners are brought in late into the research process and are not fully aware of the different stages of planning. It is more challenging if cross-functional partners come straight to the readout and question the discussion guide, interview script, survey questions, or methodology.

To navigate this oversight, it is the prerogative of the researcher to proactively reach out, if and when possible, and get cross-functional partners involved from the get-go in the research planning process.

Involving cross-functional partners early helps with the right alignment. It gives them a chance to speak up, get their questions added, and feel comfortable with the methodology.

IF YOUR PRODUCT LEADERS ASK, "WHEN IS THE RIGHT TIME TO BRING UX RESEARCH INTO THE PRODUCT CYCLE?"

Research is valuable at every stage of the product.

DISCOVERY (PRE-PROTOTYPE)

When the product doesn't yet exist: "You want to know WHAT to build."

What are people doing? How are they doing it? Why are they doing it?

Some standard methods used in the discovery phase are:

- *Ethnography*: When you want to develop an early understanding of the relevant domain, audience(s), processes, goals, and context(s) of use.
- *Diary study*: When you need to understand long-term user behavior to understand unmet needs
- *Interviews*: When you need an in-depth exploration of the interviewee's thoughts, feelings, and understanding

VALIDATION AND TESTING (PROTOTYPES)

When product designs have been created: "You want to OPTIMIZE your product" and learn if people are using the product as intended. Why (not)? What is (not) working well? What else should we consider?

Some standard methods used in the validation and testing phase:

- *Usability studies*: When you want to evaluate a prototype by having users use it
- *Participatory design*: When it is most useful to codesign with participants that express what matters to them the most and why
- *Diary studies*: When you need to understand the long-term user behavior of a product and what changes need to be made.

ONGOING LISTENING (POSTLAUNCH)

When a product gets launched: "You want to learn HOW and WHY people are using your product." How well does this solution solve the problem? What could be improved?

Some standard methods used in the postlaunch phase include:

- *Surveys*: When you want to vet the hypothesis with a larger sample
- *Usability studies*: When you want to evaluate a live product
- *Eye tracking*: When you want to precisely measure where participants look as they perform tasks or interact naturally with websites, applications, physical products, or environments.
- *Diary studies*: When you need to understand long-term user behavior of how the live product is being used.

How Early Should You Involve Your Cross-Functional Partners?

Each researcher, irrespective of if they are embedded in the product or supporting ad hoc, should involve cross-functional partners at the first instance—preferably during the research project kick-off and involve them in all the stages of the research.

Furthermore, don't stop at the main point of contact! Engage with team members from various disciplines, such as engineers, data scientists, and PMs, to get diverse perspectives and insights. By involving them in the research process, you can align on the research goal and learn early on if they have any hypotheses they are looking to test. This also helps you avoid any surprises at the end and ensure that everyone gets the insights they require.

If you are an in-house researcher embedded in the product, involve your stakeholders as early as when your draft of the research roadmap is ready. The earlier you involve them, the more accountable they become to keep you updated on any changes to the product roadmap and to leverage the findings from your research for product and design decisions.

You will find many strategies in the coming chapters on how to engage cross-functional partners early.

ANUBHAV KUSHWAHA, DIRECTOR OF ENGINEERING, DOORDASH

Several patterns emerge when I think of times when cross-functional collaboration was effective versus when it was not. A big part of success depends on the timing, structure, and continuity of involving the right partners. There is also the added nuance of considering the partners' maturity (e.g., have they worked with UX researchers in the past?) and criticality (e.g., do they have to sign off on key decisions?) when involving them.

I will share two anecdotes and a reasonable framework for partnering across the cross-functional spectrum.

First, let me share an instance when the timing and collaboration worked well. We had a senior UX researcher on my team, and they were tasked to figure out ways to simplify the experience used by internal users in the AWS supply chain. The first thing she did was to get key leaders across engineering, operations (the organization where the users were), product, and finance together with two simple questions: (1) What does it mean for you to simplify these workflows? (2) Why do you care about simplification?

This helped her identify that the main focus was not on helping users do their tasks faster but rather on reducing the number of mistakes they made, leading to incorrect decision-making down later in the process. For example, if the users incorrectly mapped a CPU to a server type, then the forecasts for how many CPUs are needed may end up being incorrect. This allowed her to anchor further research on "accuracy," which was much more focused rather than on a broader and more abstract concept of "simplification." Next, she did some quick observation sessions where she recorded the users going about their tasks using the existing tool. She made note of areas where she thought they made mistakes and then asked the more experienced users for their opinions. Hereafter she laid out a roadmap and broke it into milestones in terms of what her research would focus on, what questions she would answer, and what decisions she needed the cross-functional group to make. She kept everyone involved in the process using a cadence (biweekly syncs) and a continuous asynchronous share-out as mechanisms. This kept the entire group connected to the research and prevented big surprises or changes between the weeks. She was able to correct the course based on feedback and educate the group on insights, reasoning, etc. This ended with actionable insights and the entire group feeling that they got a lot of value from the research (and this was proven in the metrics postlaunch of the new features that were defined as an outcome of that effort).

Now where things didn't work well. This was a different project; we were looking to improve the user experience of collecting preferred drop-off locations at their properties from customers. Here also, we were lucky enough to have a senior UX researcher working with the cross-functional group. She was more tenured than several others in the group. We started with the prompt to understand the barriers for customers: why were they not giving us accurate locations when we dropped packages off at the wrong locations? After all, they must care to get their packages to the right place. This was a big problem, and there was an urgency to solve it as it impacted millions of users. Our researcher here felt she understood the problem space well and kicked off a user research survey without involving any of the cross-functional partners in defining the survey. She felt she would rather start with some well-defined pillars to break down the problem to help guide the group to a solution faster.

Further, she did not share her roadmap or thought process on how she was thinking about attacking the problem. What happened in parallel was a bit surprising to her, but in hindsight it probably shouldn't be. The product team kicked off their own user research to get ahead of the problem. We ended up with somewhat competing surveys with somewhat conflicting insights. It took several weeks for us to align from that point on building a framework and finally creating a structure to move in the right direction.

There are some clear aspects of the framework of sharing and collaboration that pop out:

Share a strawman, align on it early: Even before putting in a lot of work on the research or even the roadmap, start a skeleton and let people know about what you are thinking or planning to do. This puts you in a clear position of accountability and allows you to drive the research direction.

Understand the why behind the why: Early in the process, work with the cross-functional leaders to understand the reason they think this research is useful or important or to uncover the dimension that they are most interested in. Getting clarity on a focus area saves a lot of effort and reduces confusion.

Create a structure, and share it with clearly marked responsibilities: Whether it is a survey or the research calendar, putting it in an easy-to-understand structure and sharing it with partners helps set expectations on pace, outcomes, and where they will need to pitch in.

Build mechanisms to keep things aligned: Cadences, ownership maps of metrics/outcomes (such as RACI—responsible, accountable, consulted, and informed), asynchronous updates with tagged tasks, etc., are all good mechanisms to ensure that there is clarity of ownership, timelines, expectations, etc., across the group.

Mistake 4—Letting Cross-Functional Partners Analyze and Present the Research Findings *Without Researchers' Input*

This is an extension of the earlier thoughts. Since you are the strategic partner responsible for owning your expertise, it is your role to lead the analysis of the findings and present the insights to cross-functional partners and leadership.

As researchers, we possess numerous tools that help us remain impartial and effectively analyze data. However, cross-functional partners often bring their strong hypotheses to the table and can exhibit a bias toward findings that support their ideas and overlook insights that contradict their thought process. Moreover, they may not have the expertise to analyze thousands of lines of qualitative findings and, consequently, may misinterpret the data.

It is not uncommon for cross-functional partners to present only the insights that align with their hypothesis and use them to influence decision-making while presenting to decision-makers. This approach demonstrates confirmation bias (*the tendency to search for, interpret, favor, and recall information in a way that confirms or supports one's prior beliefs or values*), which can hinder the validity and effectiveness of research. To promote objectivity, it is crucial that the researcher presents the findings or signs off on the final presentation to ensure that all insights, both positive and negative, are conveyed.

Allow me to recount a recent positive experience I had. In this particular instance, our senior leadership requested my team to present research findings and updates on our product strategy to a substantial audience of 350 colleagues during the highly anticipated company-wide all-hands meeting.

For those unfamiliar, *all-hands meetings are company-wide meetings where the entire team, from executives to individual contributors, come together and hear updates, discuss strategic priorities, share successes, and address any concerns or questions.*

Given the time constraint of a mere ten minutes, we needed to deliver our presentation without passing the mic around like a hot potato.

During this stage, I must admit I often feel anxious and protective of research insights, as I worry that findings may be misrepresented or misinterpreted, which could potentially compromise their accuracy and validity.

To the immense credit of my PM, she afforded me complete control over the selection of research to be presented and requested that I furnish her with the precise talking points to be used. To navigate this, together with my PM, we carefully considered and selected the most impactful research findings for the presentation. Through productive and enriching discussions, wherein ideas were freely shared, we managed to distill a wealth of information into key insights that would effectively inform the entire team's product priorities and, by extension, elevate the quality of our offering.

This collaborative endeavor underscored the inherent value of fostering cross-functional partnerships, as it exemplified how such alliances are instrumental in attaining favorable and successful outcomes.

DO YOUR PRODUCT PARTNERS ASK, "HOW DO YOU ANALYZE QUALITATIVE INTERVIEW SESSIONS?"

Qualitative analysis is much more than a simple compilation of data points. Every research session is full of observations, but not every observation constitutes a useful piece of data.

Analyzing research observations is a scientific process that involves poring through data to find the most important themes. Then we make sense of those themes via frameworks. Another key point to remember is that insight doesn't have to appear 100 times to be an insight. In qualitative research, we aren't looking for our sample to be "representative," so each insight can stand on its own as long as it tells a useful story.

We essentially put an organized framework on the messiness of life.

*[**True story of a mistake I made**]—During the early days of my career, I collaborated with a new product manager on a project. Right from the outset, I made sure to keep all cross-functional partners in the loop about the research and even invited them to observe live research sessions. Since I had established a strong relationship with my cross-functional partners, I did not feel the need to set any strict rules around working with UX Research.*

After the sessions were wrapped up, I received a calendar invite, for which I was marked as "Optional," for a "Leadership Review" the next day. Since it was the day after I had finished moderating sessions, I had yet to start putting together the report. I, luckily, went to the leadership review and saw my product manager presenting the research findings based on HER analysis of watching the sessions. The most alarming part was not her analyzing the data and presenting the findings but wrongly interpreting the data.

In the concept testing, we evaluated one of the designs that had a button; pressing that played the user's favorite playlist. All participants unanimously disliked the purpose of the button, and hence my PM interpreted that the button needed to go. What she missed connecting with was the second part of the participants' feedback. The participants thought that the purpose of the button was to reset the playlist.

It is critical to understand here that participants got the intent wrong. They disliked the button when they assumed it was to reset the playlist but were actually excited when they realized it was for playing their favorite playlist. The correct insight here was to recommend to the designers to explore more ways of representing the favorite playlist interface.

This taught me a valuable lesson on setting expectations clearly and early on.

Mistake 5—Expressing Discontent When Cross-Functional Partners Do Not Leverage *Every* Insight From Research

How many times has it happened to you that the product partners did not incorporate every insight from the research report? They took some insights into consideration while paying little attention to others.

We often get disheartened when this happens and explain this behavior by thinking that the product partner does not believe in some insights, or they are exhibiting confirmation bias and only want to focus on insights they personally believe in, or they don't care for the user's needs. When in fact, sometimes it might be us—we might be overlooking the business needs and limitations and forgetting that certain insights are harder to implement. This can sometimes lead our cross-functional partners to conclude that the researcher lacks a holistic perspective or is indifferent to the business facets.

As researchers, we must always advocate for our users while also taking into consideration business goals and constraints, such as budget and technology limitations.

There can be numerous reasons why executing on a research insight could be a challenge:

- The decision-makers expect to see a **flywheel effect** (*when you see success over time*) and need to overlook immediate feedback from users. I have frequently seen this in practice. Participants dislike a new experience in a user study when it requires a new mental model or implies learning. Yet, over time, they appreciate the change and find it valuable. Nevertheless, each stakeholder should estimate the cost of losing a user or causing dissatisfaction if the experiment fails and if it is worth the risk.

- The **ROI (return on investment) is negative**—The cost of implementing is occasionally much higher than the benefit to the user or the company. Some insights require considerable investment in materials and resources and would not reap the same profits for the company. However, if the insight suggests that the user is dissatisfied, the team should reassess the trade-offs.

- **Technological limitations**—Often, the insights from research require the use of much-advanced technology, which might not be built yet.

- The **user goal and business goal conflict**—Occasionally, users may express needs that conflict with the goals of the business. An example of this is when participants convey their distaste for seeing ads. However, advertisements are a crucial source of revenue for some companies. They would shut down if they could not show ads. In these instances, research should aim to uncover insights that could reduce the level of distraction that ads pose for users, explore alternative approaches to mitigate those feelings, or find ways to make ads enjoyable.

Next time, after your research insights are ready, before drawing any judgments, sit with your cross-functional partners and discuss:

- Which insights to prioritize and implement with immediate effect?
- Which insights need to be revisited later based on product priorities?
- Which insights will not be acted upon and why?

Mistake 6—Persisting With Academic-Style Research in the Corporate World

Venturing into the corporate world is akin to decoding a new, intricate language. It's filled with novel terminologies, diverse team dynamics, and, of course, a continual stream of meetings. However, when one transitions to the industry from a doctoral degree or spends years as a lecturer or professor, it poses additional challenges, such as the practical application of research tied to business goals and communicating research reports in a more precise and efficient way.

Academic research luxuriates in theoretical constructs, experimental techniques, and statistical explorations. On the other hand, its corporate counterpart pivots toward pragmatic applications, direct relevance to user needs, and alignment with business objectives. UX researchers need to work more closely with cross-functional teams to ensure that research insights are effectively integrated into product development processes. Unlike some academic research, user research cannot scale in a vacuum, and close collaboration plays a key role.

Further, the realm of academia and a doctoral or professorial background often bestow a measured approach to research, replete with in-depth analyses, and richly detailed reports. However, the corporate landscape operates at a quicker pace, demanding rapid research without sacrificing the quality of insights and necessitating concise and effective communication of findings in a way that is easily digestible for non-research stakeholders. Individuals steeped in academia tend to transport their academic writing style into the corporate environment, producing dense and exhaustive reports. While appropriate in academia, such reports are not successful in a work setting where the attention span of the audience is limited.

In the forthcoming chapters, you will find various tactics for adapting research to business objectives, cross-functional collaboration, and crafting precise yet effective reports.

4

Simple Strategies for Effective Cross-Functional Collaboration

DOI: 10.1201/9781003391036-4

Certain strategies are time-intensive and need to be planned once or twice a year. In comparison, others work best when done frequently and consistently. The current chapter will focus on simple everyday strategies that require relatively little effort, and applying them will strengthen your cross-functional relationships and prevent you from committing the mistakes touched upon in the earlier chapter.

In this chapter, we'll cover everything from building strong relationships with cross-functional partners to evangelizing the value of UX research and making your findings easily digestible for others. We'll also delve into effective collaboration techniques and the importance of sharing insights with your team. Plus, we'll explore the benefits of acknowledging the contributions of other cross-functional partners and when it's important to be proactive and take the lead.

Build Relationships

Strong relationships foster trust, communication, and collaboration, all of which are necessary for achieving shared goals and delivering high-quality results.

Prioritizing relationship-building efforts is a foundational element of any collaborative endeavor. But the question is, how? Let's focus on some strategies that UX researchers can adopt.

Show Empathy

As researchers, empathy is second nature to us. You cannot be a good researcher if you cannot empathize with your participants. But we often reserve this empathy for our users and do not necessarily put it into action for our cross-functional partners.

There is a likelihood that your cross-functional partners have never worked with UX research in the past. Their first experience could be working with you on the job. While design courses often incorporate user research coursework, other disciplines seldom delve into user research during their education. On the other hand, even if your collaborators have worked with research extensively, there's still a possibility that their approach and experience differ from your own. Therefore, it's crucial to establish open lines of communication and a shared understanding of goals and processes to ensure successful collaboration.

"See it my way."

A good starting point is to ask a few questions when you first start working with product and design partners:

- Have you ever worked with a user researcher before? I am curious about your experience working with researchers.
- Anything in particular that helped in having a successful collaboration?
- [If supporting an ad hoc project] What are your expectations from UX research for collaboration on this project?

In summary, don't assume they know about research or how to work with researchers. Just ask.

LILLIAN CHEN, CONTENT STRATEGIST AND SR. UX DESIGNER

Although UX research is a standard discipline in many mid- to large-sized tech companies, I suspect there are those who still think having a dedicated UX researcher is a luxury rather than a necessity. But in my experience working on product teams, having someone who knows the target demographic intimately and understands how to articulate what the people want is often the difference between a team that knows what direction they're going in and a team that drifts aimlessly and spins in circles. In other words, a good UX researcher is like a team's compass, helping to keep the team on track and letting them know when they're straying too far west.

During my time as a content designer, some of my favorite partners were often UX researchers. One of my best examples of an effective partnership with a researcher came from my first team at a large tech company. As an incubator-type team, we focused on building new experiences and products for our target demographic of teens. One of our major projects was to build a messaging app for teens and their school community. It gave me many opportunities to work closely with my UX researcher and understand how our work amplified each other's work.

In the early stages of developing the app, one of the primary issues we had to solve was the "cold start" problem. We needed some sort of existing content in the app to help get things started among users, but what exactly this content should be was difficult to pinpoint. My researcher and I spent a lot of time holed up in meeting rooms, discussing all the various findings from her research work and using those insights to develop a content strategy. We would then test that strategy with our product prototype and, with each round of research, continue to analyze insights and refine the content strategy to get closer to our goal of achieving product market fit.

As it so often is with iterative work, the multiple rounds of user testing often felt like a perpetual "one step forward, two steps back" cycle, but slowly, we began to see incremental improvements in both our quantitative and qualitative data. Each tiny win felt exhilarating because we knew how much time and effort had gone into achieving our results. In our last round of research tests, when one of the teen participants said, "If you guys do this right, this app can change the world," I wanted to stand up and cheer. It was amazing to hear such unequivocally positive feedback, but it also validated how crucial and effective our partnership was as a content designer and UX researcher, not to mention the close collaboration of the entire product team.

This experience really set the gold standard for me in terms of how I wanted to work with other researchers (not to mention others) moving forward. When I look back and reflect on our collaboration, what stands out is that we were clearly aligned on our goals and worked together to create a plan and a process. In doing so, we established a strong foundation of trust and open communication, which also served us well when unexpected issues inevitably came up or when we had to pivot and figure out a new strategy. Over the course of many, many 1:1s in which we discussed all aspects of the product, shared notes on our respective areas of work, brainstormed ideas, and occasionally vented about our frustrations and challenges, we built a solid relationship that became the key to our collaboration success.

It's worth mentioning that this particular research partner of mine was also fundamentally invested in my work as well as the skills and knowledge I brought to the table. Without this as a baseline, it typically becomes much more difficult to cultivate a relationship that goes beyond a simple, transactional one. In my experience working with various user researchers, I have found that those who made little to no effort to get to know me or engage with my work often ended up struggling in a silo themselves or had a hard time getting the rest of the team engaged with their research work. It's not that building a stronger relationship with me would have single-handedly improved outcomes, but in observing how they showed up (or didn't show up) for me, it became clear that they also weren't building effective relationships with others on the team. Obviously, relationship building takes time and repeated effort. But sometimes, I think we underestimate the power of simply showing interest and curiosity in another person. Many times, I've found that phrases like, "Can you tell me more about your role?" or "I'd love to hear more" is an easy gateway to help both parties engage in a meaningful conversation, which then contributes to a stronger foundation for relationship building.

If you couldn't tell already, UX researchers are some of my favorite people to work with and are valuable partners to have on any team. They're also keen observers and listeners who tend to have a sense of humor about the idiosyncrasies of human behavior. Just ask any researcher to tell you about some of the more interesting things they've heard in their studies, and you'll gain a better appreciation for how funny we are as humans.

Set Up Regular 1:1 Meetings

Building empathy and relationships with cross-functional partners requires regular opportunities to meet and interact with them.

One major mistake I made in my early career years was forming the notion that my cross-functional partners would not benefit from meeting me outside of team meetings. Since they know about the research I am planning, I assumed there was little to share and tell. I soon realized that without 1:1 meetings with each cross-functional partner, there was no forum for them to share upcoming research needs, inform about changes in product priorities, and build a connection. I was forfeiting an easy way to have an impact.

Once I started meeting with them regularly, both they and I were more in sync, and the regular communication avoided any future pitfalls.

Further, it helped me hear from cross-functional partners who otherwise don't speak up in team settings.

These meetings also provided me with a platform to tailor and share my research findings and seek any feedback on the research plans.

Lastly, PMs manage deadlines, and keeping them aware of the research projects and time-lines is critical.

Even when collaborating as a vendor, regular 1:1s with cross-functional partners are beneficial as it provides an opportunity to probe the product space and understand it better, which in turn helps you develop a robust discussion guide or survey questionnaire. These 1:1s also help develop a camaraderie with the team, understand what kind of insights would be most valuable to the team, and keep up the team's engagement with the ongoing research.

The 1:1 meetings with cross-functional stakeholders are an important tool for building relationships, providing feedback, addressing issues, facilitating collaboration, and developing skills. They can help create a more cohesive and productive team, which benefits both you and them.

STEPHANIE KIM, CONTRACT UX RESEARCHER, INSTACART

As a contract UX researcher, I work on research projects horizontally across product teams rather than working as an embedded researcher on a team. This has its own challenges and opportunities.

This gives me a great opportunity to collaborate with various cross-functional partners and widen my understanding of the consumer journey.

On the other hand, it requires constant context switching as I am quickly onboarding different product teams and their research needs on a monthly basis. Further, I am often not allowed to attend certain strategic meetings that are reserved for embedded researchers only.

In my role a few years ago, I had a three-week research project cycle that spanned from kick-off to report presentation. When I first stepped into my role, I quickly realized that there were constraints to fully grasp the research needs within a single kick-off meeting. The research project started by syncing with the core cross-functional partners and aligning on the research needs, questions, recruitment criteria, and timeline. Since I was onboarding the team and kicking off a project at the same time, there were often gaps in my understanding of the particular product space and research needs.

I suggested to my then-manager that attending 1:1s with my cross-functional partners, such as the PM, designer, and data scientist on the team, might allow me to understand project needs better and build camaraderie. But she was hesitant, worrying that this might take too much time and it might overwhelm me to meet so many new people every three weeks.

I understood her concerns but still wanted to give this strategy a shot, and I am glad I did! These 1:1s allowed me to show up as a better research partner and provided huge value to my work. By connecting with the partners 1:1, I was able to understand the product space from different perspectives and learn how research insights can specifically support their work. Additionally, meeting the cross-functional partners 1:1 early in the process allowed us to get to know each other and build a stronger foundation for working together.

My takeaways from this experience were:

1. Don't be afraid to be proactive and find opportunities to collaborate
2. Involve cross-functional partners early in the process and build a foundation for working together
3. Approach with curiosity to learn and lean on your team's expertise (as they do with you!)

Don't Assume and Jump to Conclusions

Have your cross-functional partners ever come to you and said,

> Can we launch a survey to understand why users are not using the new feature?
>   or
> Can you plan for a concept testing study to understand concerns with the user flow for this one design?

And our first reaction is often one of frustration since perhaps survey or concept testing was not the right methodology.

In my experience, I have observed that cross-functional partners often don't mean to dictate the method research should be using and are using "survey" or "concept testing" as placeholders for research. It's common for them to use industry jargon to communicate their research objectives without having a clear understanding of what these methods entail and expect the researcher to apply the correct method.

All you need to do is understand what their research needs are and then discuss with them the best-suited research techniques. Also, take this opportunity to provide a rationale as to why their proposed method of survey or concept testing is not optimum and might not serve the intended purpose.

Not jumping to conclusions and showing empathy serves us well in such situations and keeps us from straining the relationship.

WHEN YOUR PRODUCT PARTNERS ARE WARY OF RESEARCH AND ASK "WHY DO WE WANT TO CONDUCT RESEARCH?"

Always assume they have the best intention. They might not be questioning to refute the value of research but genuinely might not know the value research provides.

Tell them, we build better products and solve bigger problems when we keep real people in mind.

But people are complex; people say things, do things, think things, and feel things, and often these don't align. We want to make sense of it all, synthesizing various data types, quantitative and qualitative, to capture meaning.

With qualitative research, the results take the form of observations, comments, thoughts, and feelings and allow you to tell a story about the participant's experience. It includes information about user behaviors, needs, desires, routines, use cases, and a variety of other information essential in designing a product that will fit into a user's life.

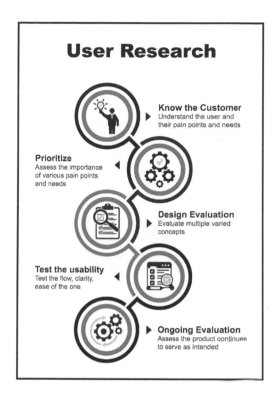

User Research

Know the Customer
Understand the user and
their pain points and needs

Prioritize
Assess the importance
of various pain points
and needs

Design Evaluation
Evaluate multiple varied
concepts

Test the usability
Test the flow, clarity,
ease of the one

Ongoing Evaluation
Assess the product continues
to serve as intended

Get Your *Foot in the Door* With a Usability Study

Establishing relationships with cross-functional partners who are unfamiliar with user research can be challenging, as they may not fully appreciate the value it brings. To address this, starting with a small but powerful step can make a big impact. Conducting a thorough usability study is an excellent way to showcase the benefits of user research and highlight its potential to inform and improve product development.

Since usability studies follow a user flow or set of designs, it is straightforward for cross-functional partners to see the value. By observing users interacting with the product, teams often discover that their initial hypothesis might not apply to every user. It inspires them to come up with different solutions and learn the value of directly learning from users.

The recommendations from usability studies are also easy to implement since they are often straightforward design changes, and it could be valuable to plan for your first study to be a usability evaluation. Once you get their buy-in and trust in research, leverage your 1:1s and team meetings to convey how research can be helpful in different stages of the product life cycle.

PRODUCT DEVELOPMENT CYCLE AND METHODS

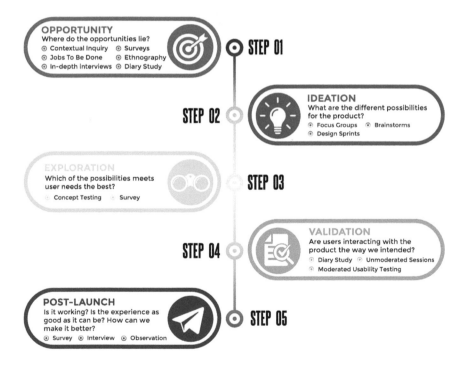

Share case studies and success stories that illustrate the impact of research on product development and proactively recommend specific studies as and when you see the product could benefit from it.

LINNEA HAGEN, RESEARCH MANAGER, AMAZON PRIME VIDEO

Customer research has a unifying power, and I wish I had taken advantage of that early and often in my career.

At most companies, people across domains (design, engineering, data, and more) want to feel and be closer to the customer, but sometimes researchers create barriers—whether they are intentional or not.

I remember early in my career, I disliked the feeling of being watched by my stake-holders and partners as I ran research—it wasn't something I was comfortable with. I felt like I was putting on a show where I had to be perfect. I would (unintentionally) create micro-barriers for partners, such as only sharing the session schedule with a limited set of key people or scheduling the sessions at times that were inconvenient for business hours (such as evenings or weekends).

My intent was not necessarily to discourage people from attending. Still, whether or not that was my intent, it's what would often happen. It took me a while to not only be comfortable being watched but embrace it. A key unlock for me was realizing nobody really paid attention to me—people were laser-focused on the customer and what they were doing. I was merely there to support them through whatever they were doing and guide the conversation/study.

Another unlock was the outcome of inviting a wide range of partners to observe research—it helped me deliver more thoughtful insights and have a far-reaching impact. My research was viewed by people working on vastly different topics who could still learn from what the customer was doing—in ways I would have never been able to know if they hadn't attended the session.

Encouraging people who were in different fields, such as engineering and finance, allowed me to have better conversations about what we could do with the insights and where we go next since engineers had creative solutions for problems from a tech perspective and finance could brainstorm success metrics and business goals.

The more researchers embrace their unifying power and embrace collaboration as a key way to get things done, the better. Most importantly, it's better for the end results for our customers—whoever they are!

⁇ DOES YOUR PM REJECT THE FINDING OF YOUR STUDY DUE TO SMALL SAMPLE SIZES?

With the plethora of log data and survey metrics we collect about our users, we often assume we understand user behavior and attitudes. Numbers, however, are just one way of learning about the world and our users. With qualitative research, we can understand the how and why of a particular issue, process, situation, or set of social interactions.

Quantitative research helps us generalize user behavior into numbers that represent broader population trends and can be tracked over time. However, these numbers do not capture all aspects—and perhaps not the most important aspects—-of a user's reality. Qualitative research enables us to understand people's motivations, behaviors, and values. In this case, a large sample size is not required. Even a small sample size is sufficient as we are trying to understand the reasons for behavior or attitude rather than its prevalence.

SCIENCE ● ● ●

Type of research design

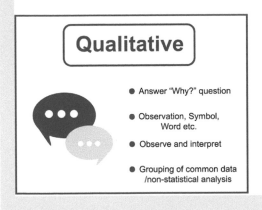

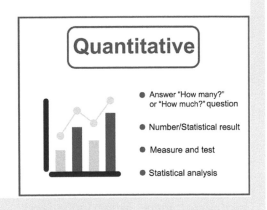

Ask Questions

You don't know what you don't know!

When you're new to a team or project, it is natural to have gaps in your familiarity and understanding of the product. You don't know what you don't know, and you would not know unless someone else tells you or helps you. The best way to overcome this challenge is to be proactive in seeking information and resources.

One way to do this is by asking questions and being transparent about what you don't know. Don't be afraid to reach out to your team members and ask for help. Request to be added to relevant meetings and discussions so that you can learn more about the product vision and understand how your work fits into the bigger picture.

Another approach is to ask them to share any data or documents that might help you better understand the product or project. For example, if there are analytics reports or insights from beta testing that provide insights into user behavior, make sure to ask for them.

Finally, seek out recommendations from your team members on how to best share your own research and insights for maximum impact.

If you are hesitant to ask any of these questions or struggle to find the right answers, active listening and running prioritization exercises can help.

TODD CARMODY, CONSULTANT, RESEARCH STRATEGY LEAD

ACTIVE LISTENING: UX RESEARCH FROM THE CONSULTANT'S PERSPECTIVE

The meeting had been on the books—someone's books—for months. But our team of external consultants, hard at work on what we now realized was just one of four work streams in a much larger project, had only recently been invited to attend. From a project management perspective, we had all the information we needed: who would be at the meeting and what they would be sharing. From a strategic perspective, though, we found ourselves at a distinct disadvantage. We hadn't had a chance to understand how the moving parts fit together or what—from this more holistic vantage—the most important unknowns and opportunities actually are. It's hard to show up for your research when you're no longer sure where the playing field is.

Moments like this are far from rare for UX researchers working in consultancies or agencies. By definition, not being in-house means not having a complete picture of the broader context that clients are working with. This broader context might include the end-to-end product life cycle or the business decisions your research could potentially be used to justify (or veto). The parable of "the blind man and the elephant"—feeling around for a sense of the whole inch by inch—has its parallels here. Being "out of the house," however, can also be a superpower. Clients hire consultants precisely because they want a fresh perspective, one not bogged down by internal preconceptions (or politics). As an external UXer, the challenge is thus making good on your superpower—using your research to influence the decisions made by client teams and stakeholders without necessarily having all the information all the time.

But how do you do this? The easy answer is also the least satisfying: UX researchers who work in consultancies and agencies are, of necessity, great listeners, blessed with or quick to learn the soft skills of intuiting what clients are *really* saying or what they *really* want. These skills come with experience, of course. The more projects you have under your belt—and even better, the more projects with a particular client—the sharper your understanding of the organizational contexts, stakes, and pitfalls that matter most. But there are also a number of practical, actionable strategies that can help you advocate for your research as a thought partner and influence cross-functional partners.

In what follows, I'm going to outline a few such strategies to get you started. Technically, these strategies fall under the umbrella of "prioritization exercise" (more on that term below). But to get yourself oriented to the bigger picture, it's also helpful to think of these exercises more broadly as tools for "active listening." By active listening, I mean actively creating opportunities to listen closely and learn more about what clients or stakeholders have in mind. These methods are particularly useful when you don't feel it would be appropriate to ask outright or—and this happens just as frequently—you don't know yet which questions would be best to ask. Think about active listening as a way to gather intelligence that will help you be a better thought partner, adviser, and even sparring partner for your clients. At base, the goal is to understand the assumptions, expectations, and aspirations that have not yet been made explicit. These will include both "known unknowns" (questions that are already top of mind for you) and "unknown unknowns" (questions that haven't yet been on your radar but probably should have been).

ACTIVE LISTENING WITH PRIORITIZATION EXERCISES

The term "prioritization exercise" can be used to describe any activity where you work together with clients to sort a given number of items on a predetermined list along a spectrum leading from least to most desirable. The items might be product features, research approaches, or markets—anything where you've got more options than you can actually pursue and need to determine where to focus your efforts and budget. There are many different ways to structure prioritization exercises, but it's useful to think of them as belonging to one of two categories: informal and formal prioritization exercises.

Informal prioritization exercises: sharing material with the client in advance of regularly scheduled meetings in order to "take the temperature of the room" and see what generates the most excitement. Useful at every stage of a project.

Think of every interaction with a client as an informal prioritization exercise. Whether casually swapping ideas or sharing learnings from the research at hand, everything you discuss with the client is a chance to understand where their thinking is heading. It's best, though, to build in regular opportunities to put material in front of the client on an informal basis. What kinds of exchanges work best will vary from client to client and from project to project, but also on your team's working style. Here are a few options to consider:

- *Regularly updated website*: Set up an internal website or knowledge-sharing platform to provide regular "drips" of content, information, insights, and/or perspectives throughout the life of the project and develop some system for gathering feedback along the way. The latter might be a commenting function, but it might also be a regular meeting where you revisit what has been posted on the website while conducting other business.

- *"Postcards from the field"*: This can be a deck that you regularly update with individual perspectives garnered during the course of research. They might be profiles of users along with their user journeys or summaries of expert interviews with a brief introduction to the people you've spoken with.

- *Weekly tracker deck*: Let's assume that you're meeting once a week with the client to update them on your progress and resolve logistical issues. You'll usually need a slide deck of some sort to do this. When it comes to prioritization, it can be useful to use the same deck from one week to the next, adding an overview of each meeting and new content as you go along. By keeping the conversation cumulative in this way, you can establish a shared sense of purpose and strategy. But you can also track how clients see the relationship between what you're sharing for the first time and what you've shared in the past weeks. The type of content is up to you—emerging insights, adjacent perspectives, provocative developments in related fields—but the goal is always the same: See what you can learn about what else is shaping clients' thinking on the question at hand.

- *Formal prioritization exercises*: Engaging with clients in a workshop-type setting with an agenda organized specifically to build consensus around a well-defined question. These exercises are generally held at pivotal moments in a project—when moving from one phase to another, where a decision is required to advance, or at the end of a project, or to build consensus around a conclusion that has already been reached.

These formal prioritization exercises should be built into the project design from the beginning of the project. Your team and the client team will then operate with a sense of direction, moving through the research with the understanding that you will be able to recalibrate the strategic direction before the next stage of the project begins. There are many ways to organize these formal prioritization exercises, but here are two.

- *2×2 prioritization matrix*: A 2×2 prioritization matrix is a simple but powerful tool prioritizing predetermined inputs—features, ideas, or requirements—based on two key criteria. The two criteria used in the matrix can vary depending on the context, but it can be useful to start with IMPORTANCE and URGENCY as the x and y-axes, where importance is the potential impact on user experience or business goals and urgency is the deadline or level of associated risk. The resulting matrix is made up of four quadrants, each representing a different priority level. You can then sort your inputs—product designs, potential new markets, and user needs—into one of the four quadrants. If IMPORTANCE and URGENCY are your axes, the quadrants will be (1) highly important and urgent, (2) important but not urgent, (3) urgent but not important, and (4) neither important nor urgent. Tasks in quadrant 1 should be prioritized over those in quadrant 2, and so on down the list.

- *MoSCow method*: A MoSCoW exercise is also a technique for prioritizing project inputs or requirements based on their level of importance or urgency. The acronym "MoSCoW" stands for must have, should have, could have, and won't have. During the exercise, your team will work together with clients to assign each input to one of these four categories. Once all the requirements have been categorized, the team can then focus on the must-have and should-have inputs first and then move on to the could-have inputs if time and resources allow. The won't-have inputs are excluded from the project scope.

- *Heart-head-pirate prioritization*: This technique is used to prioritize inputs based on three different criteria: emotional appeal (heart), rational value (head), and business value (pirate). During the exercise, work with the client team to rate each feature or requirement on each of the three criteria, using a scale from 1 to 5. Once all the features have been rated, the scores are added up for each criterion, and the features are then prioritized based on their total scores.

Using a combination of informal and formal prioritization exercises in your work as an external UX researcher will help you understand the kinds of background information, assumptions, and ambitions that are driving client expectations but that might never be explicitly stated as such. Ultimately, these techniques are opportunities for active listening that help outside consultants—and anyone else who finds themselves without the full picture of what's going on—ensure their research is as impactful as possible.

Level Up Your Impact by Showing Up and Being Present

Optics Matter!

Every product is built by the joint efforts of multiple disciplines that regularly meet to support and collaborate with each other. While this is not an exhaustive list, these meetings usually include:

- *Team meeting*: Cross-functional partners meet to share updates and discuss priorities
- *Stand-ups*: Mostly led by engineering, where daily updates are shared
- *Product reviews*: The team meets with the leadership to discuss progress and roadblocks and seek advice
- *Demos*: Engineers and designers showcase the latest designs, flows, and the built phases of the product

The cadence for different types of meetings varies based on the organization and product deadlines.

While the presence of UX research is often optional for most of these meetings, making time and effort to show up when the schedule permits can prove beneficial. Attending these meetings helps you understand the team priorities and adjust research priorities accordingly. Moreover, a researcher's presence in these meetings can remind cross-functional partners that research can support all stages of a product cycle, build strong partnerships, and reinforce the notion that research is always there to help.

If you are an external vendor or consultant, you might not be approved to sit in these meetings. In that case, seek permission to get added to a few of these meetings or leverage your 1:1s to get a run-through of any decisions being made in these meetings that impact your project. You may need to add this to the standing 1:1 agenda to ensure you are up-to-date with all the latest updates.

The only caveat, though, here is that "Don't be a warm body." Being a warm body in a meeting means simply showing up physically but not contributing to the discussion or providing any meaningful input. It's important to come prepared, have a clear understanding of the meeting's purpose and objectives, and actively engage. This can include asking thoughtful questions, sharing relevant information or ideas, and attentively listening to others.

Do not just attend meetings but also make the time and effort to comment on product requirement documents (PRD). Provide any relevant research insights that can help inform the team's decision-making process.

Product requirement documents (PRD) outline the requirements and specifications for a particular product or feature and typically include detailed information about the product's functionality, features, and user interface, as well as any technical requirements or constraints.

Evangelize UX Research and Research Processes

UX research provides valuable insights into user behavior, preferences, and pain points, which can help to inform design decisions and improve the overall user experience.

By promoting UX research, you can help to build a culture of user-centric design within your organization. This involves advocating for the use of research in the design process, educating stakeholders about the benefits of user research, and involving them in the research process where possible.

Share UX Research 101

This relates to the "show empathy" strategy shared earlier. Irrespective of what the experience of a cross-functional partner is with research, in my experience, taking time to share what a user experience researcher does, your focus areas, the value of foundational and evaluative work, and a brief on different methodologies are always valuable.

The initial introduction with the cross-functional partner is also a fitting time to share what research timelines look like—timelines for getting approvals, timelines for executing the study, and timelines for analyzing data and presenting the report.

In some organizations, the end-to-end research finishes within a month or less, while in others, research needs to seek approvals, such as privacy and legal, before executing the study, which can increase the turnaround time to up to three months.

Another area where expectations are mismatched is the delivery time for the final report. Cross-functional partners often assume that once the study is complete, the report will be ready in a day or two. The analysis takes time, and it is important to communicate this to our project partners.

If you are an external vendor or consultant, getting a sense of client understanding and experience with UX research can provide great context on how to communicate with your client. For instance, if research is a new concept for them, more context-setting and explanation may be required. This may include clarifying the process, the limitations of research, and the justification behind certain decisions, such as small sample sizes or survey constraints.

WHEN YOUR ENGINEERING PARTNER ASKS—WHAT EXACTLY IS UX RESEARCH?

UX Research is a scientific method for understanding and empathizing with people. It is a set of processes and frameworks for

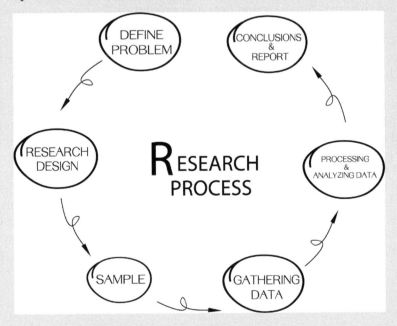

- Identifying and challenging our assumptions
- Finding commonalities and differences across our target audience
- Recognizing user needs, pain points, desires, goals, and mental models

OMER MUZAFFAR, PRODUCT MANAGER LEAD, META

As a PM for digital consumer products and experiences, I've had the opportunity to work on multiple 0–1 product (*0 to 1 means creating something completely new that didn't exist before*). What makes building these 0–1 products fun (and also hard!) is the level of ambiguity about what the real market needs are and what solutions best address those needs. You'll often find that different stakeholders come with their own perspectives, biases, and convictions about specific ideas (or not) based on their own individual experiences. This can make it challenging for everyone to align on a common understanding of the problem and opportunities and focus on a strategic direction.

User research is key to shifting from this ambiguity to clarity and consensus on target users, their needs, and solutions.

One of the 0–1 product I worked on was a voice-forward smart display. The device introduced a new voice-forward interaction paradigm, and a big challenge for us was to figure out how to teach users about what they could do. We had lots of ideas on the team (including specific asks from the executive level), but we were missing the insights about our customers to help us figure out what would or wouldn't work. Fortunately, we had an engaged UX research partner who understood the customer problem early and came to the table with unique insights about our customers— what does a day in their life look like? What are the moments in their lives where we can get their attention? What are their preferences for how and when to learn?

Having answers to some of these questions early on helped us turn a wide range of ideas into a thoughtful plan that ultimately delivered meaningful results. Without an engaged UX research partner who owned and understood the problem early and proactively shared these insights, we likely wouldn't have achieved the same outcomes.

The two simple but effective behaviors that the researcher displayed that helped increase the effectiveness of this product development process were:

- *Engaging proactively, early, and often:* She did not assume that everyone on the project fully understood the value of UX research or how to leverage it. A key part of her role was to educate partners to help them understand what meaningful insights she could bring to the table and how those could help increase the odds of success for the outcomes they were trying to drive. Simple tactics such as proactively introducing herself, driving discussions to align on key questions to answer, what tactics she plans to use to get those answers, delivering meaningful insights quickly, and regularly following up worked well.
- *Owning the problem:* Instead of thinking of her job as a support function, she internalized and thought of her role as a strategic function. Her mission was not just to deliver a research report (or other artifacts) but to drive specific outcomes to help solve a business problem.

Clarify Different Kinds of Research and Research Methods

When you are sharing all about UX research and setting expectations, another helpful expectation to set is the kind of research you would do. Since insights from evaluative studies are straightforward to implement, cross-functional partners might only seek evaluative studies. It is essential to educate cross-functional partners on the importance of foundational research and communicate that you may conduct such studies to inform the product roadmap.

Further, emphasizing that different methods have different timelines is also critical. For example, ethnographic studies may require several months to gather comprehensive data, while usability studies can be conducted and completed within a week or two. Understanding these varying timelines and communicating them to cross-functional partners can help manage their expectations and demonstrate the value of each type of research.

Another clarification often needed is when to go to UX research versus market research. Both terms are often used interchangeably since they often use similar research methodologies, but both have different expertise and goals.

If we are designing a new product or service or looking to improve an existing one, UX research is key to understanding our users and creating a product that meets their needs. On the other hand, if we are looking to launch a new product or enter a new market, market research can help us understand the competitive landscape and identify opportunities.

ⓘ WHEN SHOULD YOU APPLY MARKET RESEARCH VERSUS USER EXPERIENCE RESEARCH?

Market research is typically used to understand the broader market landscape and consumer trends, while UX research is focused on understanding how users interact with a specific product or service.

Market research can answer questions related to target customers, market size, and competition. It often involves methods such as surveys and focus groups. On the other hand, UX research can answer questions related to how users perform specific tasks within a product or service, their pain points and frustrations, and what features or functionality are most valuable to them. It typically involves methods such as user interviews, usability testing, and observational studies.

Set Expectations

Work relationships succeed when clear expectations are set on all sides from the beginning. The concern is these expectations are rarely explicitly set.

To avoid any misunderstandings, it is critical to let your cross-functional partners know about the dos and don'ts of working with research. They might not even realize they might be trespassing and unintentionally driving the work for you or might misinterpret your role.

For instance, they should collaborate with you throughout the research project but not dictate what methodology to use or how many participants to recruit. Similarly, while co-analysis of data is encouraged, your partners should refrain from interpreting the data on their own and presenting their interpretation to leadership without your input.

If you are a vendor or anyone not embedded in the team, you might need to set expectations so as not to end up re-doing what could have been avoided by setting some early expectations. Ask your cross-functional partners:

- What kind of template do they prefer?
- What formats are needed?
- What kind of recommendations and highlight reels are most impactful?

One main challenge, mostly faced by external vendors and consultants, is the request to include ad hoc questions in a current study that may or may not be related to the study objective. This can compromise the quality of the study and also divert the researcher from getting quality insights on the main topic. Setting clear expectations around this can help prevent last-minute surprises for both the researcher and the cross-functional partner.

Create Formal Processes for Research Intake

While setting expectations, you also need to set processes for research intake from cross-functional partners.

As an in-house researcher, one of the main challenges is the constant influx of ad hoc project requests that disrupt the current research schedule and make it difficult to manage cross-functional partner expectations. One of the ways to solve it is to have a robust research roadmap detailing topics you will be studying in the next 3–6 months and the corresponding timelines (*read more on roadmaps in Chapter 5*).

However, no matter how robust your roadmap is, there will always be ad hoc requests due to changing business priorities, and you need to accommodate them. The goal is to make it as least disruptive as possible.

First, you need to make sure your roadmap has the wiggle room to make some of these ad hoc requests happen. Second, decide which of the many requests you need to prioritize.

Having a formal process for research intake has always worked well for me. I ask my cross-functional partners to fill out a brief questionnaire detailing the need for the study and the impact this will have. The information helps me assess the urgency and impact and makes the cross-functional partners more thoughtful in reaching out. A little bit of effort upfront on this form from cross-functional partners helps provide more clarity on how to support the team best and manage the incoming research requests to have a more significant impact.

Setting up **UX research office hours** can also aid in making time and space for collaboration. UX research office hour is a regular hold on the team calendar where cross-functional partners have a pre-allocated and dedicated time to reach out to research and bring any open questions, dive deep into upcoming research requests, or any other requests they may have. This time can also be used to discuss any ad hoc intake request forms they might have filled out.

Research In-Take

Please note that fieldwork takes roughly one month from the start (recruitment) to completion (presentation of deliverables). Survey work takes 2-3 weeks.

Thank you for taking the time to fill out this form! Please reach out to [Researcher Name] if you have any questions.

What are the research goals/objectives? *

Short answer text

Why are you requesting research? (Please provide some background) *

Short answer text

What are some specific questions you want to be answered? *

Short answer text

What impact will it have? What decisions/product changes will be made due to the outcome * of this work?

Short answer text

In order to be actionable, when do you need results? *

Short answer text

Any links or docs that you would like to attach with the request? *

⬆ Add file   ▲ View folder

Encourage Shared Responsibility Through Active Participation

Even when cross-functional partners are eager to engage and participate in research, a challenge they encounter is a lack of understanding regarding how they can become involved and the specific actions they can take. We may spend a lot of time explaining UX research and research frameworks that are useful, but it would be ultimately incomplete if we did not explain how team members without a research background can actively participate in the research process.

"Great plan. Could we get some more details?"

Involve Cross-Functional Partners Early and in the Entire Process

There is no better alternative to increasing empathy than involving cross-functional partners in the entire research process, allowing them to experience it firsthand. This includes involvement in designing the study, co-defining objectives and recruitment criteria, analyzing the findings, and ultimately sharing the results widely. There needs to be co-ownership and accountability from everyone. Keep your cross-functional partners informed and ask for feedback throughout the research project.

Involving cross-functional partners in the research project also provides researchers with a broader perspective and may enrich their findings and thoughts.

What does it mean to involve them early?

- Partner with cross-functional team members **as soon as you start planning your particular research project**. Often you might not even know your cross-functional team, and you might be only aware of the PM or the designer involved. Ask them about other team members—engineers, content strategists, etc. The sooner you meet everyone and get their buy-in, the higher the chances of success and impact, and the fewer the chances of any thrash later.

- Get clarity on the background of the product, any past efforts to launch it, and any past decisions or data. The more you know about the product and how the team is thinking about it, the short- and long-term plans, and the end goal, the more robust your research plan will be.

- Share the research plan highlighting research questions, methodology, timelines, and past research to align on shared goals. Seek comments and feedback, as it helps ensure that everyone is on the same page and allows cross-functional partners to voice any concerns sooner than later. Similarly, seek input on the participant recruiting criteria to ensure the criteria align well with the objective of the research.

- If the methodology allows, encourage team members to observe live sessions and hear directly from the participants.

If you are an in-house researcher embedded in the team, reach out to cross-functional partners **when they are putting together product roadmaps** to seek any open questions they may have and see if a literature review of past studies can aid them in providing direction.

A product roadmap is a high-level visual summary that outlines the strategic direction and goals for a product over a specific period of time, typically 6–12 months or longer. It is a planning tool used by product managers and other stakeholders to communicate the vision, priorities, and timeline for a product's development.

Once the product roadmap is ready, **create a draft of the research roadmap** that aligns with the product roadmap **and seek early feedback from cross-functional partners**. Prioritize projects with the highest impact that can be realistically supported by the researcher. This provides clarity to cross-functional partners regarding projects where research will answer strategic questions or provide feedback on designs. This also helps them align on projects that research will not be able to support, and they need to seek alternate ways of seeking data and making decisions.

ALI HOROWITZ, CONTENT DESIGNER, META

Who's in charge of the language used in your product? (Think headers, explanations, button labels, and anything that users read and that comes from product design rather than user-generated content.) Sometimes a product designer or another role on the team—maybe you!—takes this on, but if you're really fortunate, your team will have a dedicated content designer, such as me, whose full-time job is to develop the patterns, style, and tone of communication throughout your product.

Language in prototypes shapes understanding and sentiment. Sometimes words feel so natural that they're hardly noticed! This is good for our product experience and good for our research. We feel confident that the experience is intuitive when prototypes are so straightforward that they speak for themselves.

Whenever we are conducting evaluative research, it's important to use strong content because (1) we can get user feedback on the realistic product experience and (2) participants may misinterpret or get distracted by content that's off, whether it's lorem ipsum or other placeholder text. It's a myth that "people don't read." Language matters, and participants latch onto any text they can when giving feedback!

Integrating content design early saves the team time in the long run. When the content design is not included in the creation of prototypes and study materials, we end up eating up precious session time explaining to participants what to pay attention to and what to ignore. It's a missed opportunity to get feedback on language and maximize the impact of qualitative research.

As a content designer, I work closely with my UX research partners to make sure any study materials have solid, representative content to get a signal on what's working or what stands out. I've also learned how valuable it is to test multiple versions of content with users, especially to gauge what information is necessary versus superfluous.

For example, designing for new experiences sometimes starts from a place of overexplaining with lots of labels and text on the page when a simpler version with less text is more straightforward. Getting feedback on a scale of options, from minimal words to maximal context and across different tones and framing, can help determine the Goldilocks outcome for what's just right.

Content designers love words, but we love slashing unnecessary words even more!

Bring in your content design partners early and often. They are strategic partners who have a wealth of knowledge about how language is used in a product, how concepts may tie together across experiences, and may even be able to provide insightful feedback to help improve study questions and generate more impactful insights for your team.

WYATT STAROSTA, DIRECTOR, UX RESEARCH

Involving cross-functional partners early may not always be an option when they are new to your team or are just reluctant to any qualitative insights. However, none of this should take precedence over user needs.

A few years back, I was heading the research team, and during a team lunch with designers and researchers, we were sharing stories of what was new in the growing organization. One of our junior designers reluctantly shared that she was having some issues with a recently hired PM; we'll call him Greg. Greg had joined the company after having extensive experience with one of the big management consulting firms; he was brought in to revamp our loyalty program, which was beloved by our most passionate customers for over a decade. In truth, the program was a loss leader that cost the company millions per year. Roughly $250K of that expense was due to postage, as we were physically mailing out $20 redemption checks!

Greg had proposed a new program, a digital redemption that would save the company money and, on paper, would provide greater utility and delight to the customer. He had the designer mock-up screens of the new experience and wanted to roll out the changes in the next release.

However, earlier, we had learned during research that these checks represented more than the $20 value to our customers; they were a source of pride—and in many cases, we saw stacks of them stuck to their refrigerator or stashed away in a special envelope. The designer knew that any change to the program would be met with skepticism from these loyal customers.

Our designer intuitively sensed that our core users would miss the tangibility of those checks, and more importantly, we were not disclosing those changes until after the program had rolled out. She raised the issue, but her empathy and intuition were no match for Greg's data-backed hypothesis. He was eager to make his mark.

I met with Greg, and it was awkward at first. I, too, was overwhelmed by his data. His strength was his ability to analyze and move quickly. Rather than go toe-to-toe with quantitative data, I turned the conversation to our customers. I pulled up a few video clips of recent customer visits. Greg saw the users talk passionately about the existing program, and when he saw how their faces lit up when they showed us their trove of unredeemed checks, he wanted to know more about this behavior. I proposed a quick usability/concept test of the new program, and he agreed, though I think it was more to placate the design team and not make waves as a new PM. As part of the agreement, we wouldn't push out the timeline, which meant we had two weeks to recruit and field. We pulled it off, and to his credit, Greg attended every single session. By the end of the first session, Greg's demeanor had changed. He wasn't hearing pushback from the design team. He was hearing straight from our most loyal customers. They didn't argue about the benefits of the new system. They grieved the loss of the old system and felt "tricked" because the switch to the new system caught them off guard. By the end of the seventh session, Greg decided to pause the rollout. He came to the conclusion that such an abrupt change would cause more reputational and brand harm than any perceived benefit or cost savings. He pivoted and began working on a robust communication strategy to slowly roll out the new program with input from our most loyal customers.

From that point on, Greg was hooked. He saw the research team as a way to quickly get feedback from customers to inform his decision-making. By the next planning cycle, he and the research team were enmeshed, albeit with an evaluative focus. It wasn't long before we were partnering on strategic programs, helping Greg understand new customers and behaviors so he could develop his hypothesis. Over the years, Greg became a huge advocate, and he helped the research team understand a PM's need for intuition and data.

This type of trust and cooperation wasn't handed to us. We had to cultivate it with small, quick programs that provided visceral insights that would never happen with surveys or analytics.

Similar to keeping cross-functional partners involved in the entire process, seeking their input in the analysis is also valuable. You can invite them to go through all the data together and involve them in a thematic grouping or affinity mapping. Alternatively, if this is a big ask, sharing an early draft of the report is also very effective. Early sharing helps in getting a sense of which insights speak to them and where they want more clarification.

Join Forces With Other Data and Content Partners

One of the biggest gaps I see is the lack of partnership between UX research and data science/data analysts, as well as between UX research and content design. This disconnect often stems from a lack of understanding about how these teams can collaborate to create a powerhouse of information for making product decisions.

Partner with data scientist/data analyst: When a product is launched, data science, as the name suggests, provides us with user data and trends. UX research seeks qualitative and quantitative data and provides the rationale behind the trends that data science is observing. By partnering closely at all stages of product development, data science and UX research can create a powerful feedback loop that strengthens the research data and findings. This approach can provide leadership with a comprehensive 360-degree view of the data, helping them make informed decisions with a single source of truth.

In one of my research projects working on a chat app, we inquired of participants if there was one thing they would want to change or improve in the product. The majority of participants expressed their displeasure with the 200-friend limit, citing it as a constraint that unnecessarily restricts their experience. However, rather than solely relying on this feedback, we collaborated with our data science partners to analyze the data. We discovered that 90% of the participants had only 10–12 friends IN TOTAL! way less than the limit, which indicated that the earlier qualitative feedback was not representative of the actual state of affairs.

All data sources come with their limitations, whether it be qualitative research or data analytics. This contradictory data from my case highlights how crucial it is to consider all available data before drawing any conclusions. It also emphasizes the importance of looking at user needs, behaviors, and pain points from all perspectives to find the truth, the whole truth, and nothing but the truth.

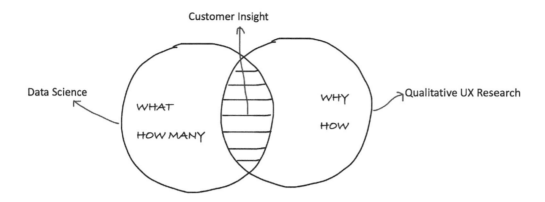

If you are a quant researcher, here is some great advice from Saeideh Bakshi, a veteran quant researcher and a dear friend:

Quantitative UX researchers and data analysts sometimes have overlapping scopes and responsibilities. Depending on the project and the needs, it is important to proactively communicate with data analysts on your team about how you want to approach the work, what is the best way to divide responsibilities, and how to collaborate. In the past, for example, as a quant, I have taken the responsibility of designing, running, and analyzing product surveys to gather self-reported data, and the product analyst has analyzed the usage logs to make sense of behaviors. Together, we collaborated to triangulate data, create compelling stories, and make recommendations for products and strategies.

In another role and project, I worked with a data analyst, and we both ran large-scale surveys, where she focused on running surveys internally with existing users through internal survey platforms and I targeted nonusers externally and again together to contribute a more holistic view of the problem by triangulating insights.

KYLE BRADY, SR. UX RESEARCHER, INSTACART

You've probably seen Christian Rohrer's research methods two-by-two chart. If you haven't, it plots user experience research methods along two axes, ranging from attitudinal to behavioral on the Y-axis and qualitative (qual) to quantitative (quant) on the X-axis. In my experience, most user researchers understand how important it is to triangulate data to create a compelling story—marrying qual with quant or pitting users' stated behavior against their observed behavior.

It's also my experience that most user researchers spend their time in the attitudinal space (guilty), popping their heads up into the behavioral realm from time to time with usability testing—maybe going so far as trawling around Google Analytics or FullStory. The problem is most user researchers aren't best equipped to explore large sets of log data, or set up product experiments and track how they impact metrics, or run complex causal analyses. However, these methods—and the insights they can generate about natural user behavior—are a powerful complement to user research. The good news is you probably already have a partner that can help.

For the first part of my career as a user researcher, I either didn't have access to or was unaware of a data science team in the organizations in which I worked. My studies built on the organizations' previous UX research work and would sometimes include external data to bolster insights. This often made translating insights into product changes a hard sell, given the smaller sample size of some studies and the self-reported nature of others. I then landed a job on the growth marketing team at a small SaaS (*software as a service*) start-up, where I had my first experience collaborating with data science.

Our team was responsible for getting prospective customers to our marketing site, sold on the value we offered through checkout, and onboarded into the product. We knew prospective customers were having trouble across these different stages—based on feedback from our salespeople and customer service representatives—but we weren't exactly sure where to start. We could do usability testing to identify pain points in the checkout process, or conduct a set of interviews to determine the hierarchy of how we presented our product features, or use countless other approaches. Or, we could consult with our data science partner, which we did.

They helped us find exactly where the drop-off was occurring at each stage of the funnel, down to the page, and—once we had done our research—worked with us to set up experiments based on our proposed design changes. Without data scientists, we would have been shooting in the dark and testing designs with a much lower probability of having any significant impact. These are just two of the ways user researchers can benefit from a partnership with data scientists. Since then, I've identified a handful of ways to collaborate with data scientists that have been most impactful to both my work and their work:

- *Hypothesis testing findings from user research with data*: This is probably what most people think when they think of collaborating with data scientists. It's great to be able to either lend weight to your insights or accept your null hypothesis and move on to other explorations. This is a powerful way to triangulate insights, but **please** do not make this the only way you collaborate with data scientists. It will make your relationship feel transactional and brittle.

- *Understanding the why behind data*: This is one of the collaborations I identified in the example above, and it is a great relationship starter: "Hey, DS, you have some interesting behavioral data, but you don't know why people are behaving that way? Let us help." Supporting data science in this way puts the value of user research on display and is—in my experience—one of the best ways to start cultivating a collaborative relationship between the two functions. It also leads really nicely into my next recommendation.

- *Create a joint user research and data science roadmap*: Both user research and data science are "understand" functions. Our functions may be different, but they are very complementary and ultimately try to accomplish the same thing: We investigate what is happening, why that thing is happening, and give recommendations as to how the company might change that thing for the better. By collaboratively planning what questions to tackle over a quarter, half, or year, you are set up to identify problems better, ask better questions, and determine better recommendations to move your company forward.

Your partners in the product are great. Your partners in design are great. But when it comes to both getting the best picture of natural user behavior and triangulating that data with user research insights, there is no better partner than data science.

SEAN RYAN, SR. UX RESEARCHER, GOOGLE

Working with data science was a bit of an enigma for me when I first started at a large tech company with a lot of data on its users. All I knew was there was a lot of talk about metrics such as DAU (daily active users) and MAU (monthly active users). And these tended to dominate a lot of conversations in leadership meetings. But there was not a clear path for me in working with data scientists directly or understanding how to tap into this pool of data.

I did not know Sequel or possess any programming or database skills. I had worked with others in the past who spoke this language, but it was definitely not something that intersected with my core work directly as a qualitative researcher.

And at this tech company, I had very light interactions with data scientists for my first few years. On my first product team, I worked with a data scientist who helped me run queries to target users in a particular geography to reach out for recruitment in qualitative research. This was very basic stuff that no data scientist is thrilled to do (and in fact, some were reluctant to do this kind of work, which was completely understandable). So, in other words, running queries for qualitative recruitment purposes was a big help to me and really only me. This relationship was mismatched in that there was not a lot of mutual help and benefit for the data scientist.

Finally, by year 3 at this same tech company, I landed on a different product team where the data scientist was a much more active thought partner with me. It was a wonderful relationship because I finally understood that while data scientists were great at building dashboards for watching metrics, they lacked the user context and answers for some of the "but, why" questions that we, as qualitative researchers, are so good at answering at times.

We really hit it off when it was clear that one of our core products was on the chopping block, and we were trying to make a case for its continued utility value to the user based on the daily activation numbers alone. But the team didn't know what the actual value was in terms of the product experience since it was just the mobile site version of the core product. So, in other words, they didn't know "why" people actually went to this mobile site and decided to use it in this way. I ended up doing a jobs-to-be-done framework to highlight the value that this product held for users. This helped confirm what the data scientist had suspected about the core values and user needs but didn't have the user context.

My key takeaways from this experience were:

- It's not always obvious how different skill areas can work together and support each other's work. But with the right question, it can become much more clear.

- Working together might mean supporting each other at first, but the greater goal is overall understanding. Data scientists and UX researchers who understand this relationship can have much more fruitful collaborations.
- Data science numbers can tell a much stronger story when the context of use is well understood. This should be the way to develop relationships between data science and UX research.

Leverage fishfood and dogfood data: Similar to data science, collaborate with partners who lead fishfooding and dogfooding efforts. When the product is being built, organizations leverage fishfooding data (*testing of new features by the immediate team that built it*) and dogfooding data (*testing of new features by the company's employees before it is launched*) to test the product. Fishfooding and dogfooding are essential tools in organizations for testing and improving products and services and provide valuable early signals to improve the product—they are akin to a usability study conducted on employees.

By leveraging the data collected from these methods, you can make more informed decisions and prioritize research on the most significant product improvements.

Enhance interview scripts with content designers' expertise: While we know (and have extensively discussed) how research can benefit product development, we often overlook the potential of orthogonal collaboration. Partnering with our content specialists can significantly enhance the quality and effectiveness of our interview scripts, screeners, and survey scripts.

KEVIN MENDOZA, SR. CONTENT DESIGNER, INSTACART

If a content designer, such as myself, is on your team, take advantage of their skills. Like most teammates, they'll want to help ensure the success of your research. Ask them to take a look at the materials you're preparing—especially if they'll be put in front of customers. It's hard to edit oneself. You're often blind to grammatical errors because you've been looking at the words you've written countless times. And you're probably too close to the subject matter to have an objective viewpoint. At a minimum, ask your content designer to do a quick sanity check. They'll review your materials with a fresh eye.

Content designers are trained to use language that resonates best with your company's users. And oftentimes, that means the microcopy seen in an app or as part of testing relies on common, everyday words that customers say naturally in conversation. For example, a word like "alternative" in an e-commerce app may come across as being a bit technical. So your content designer may suggest using a term like "similar item" instead.

I have observed several instances where my involvement as a content designer could have greatly benefited research projects, particularly in unmoderated testing where the opportunity to paraphrase a question does not exist if the questions are poorly written or are difficult to understand. Even worse, sloppiness can negatively affect people's perceptions of the company.

If you think your content designer can help you, don't hesitate to ask. I'm pretty sure they'll gladly do what they can. I definitely do!

Communicate and (Sometimes) Overcommunicate

As insightful as the "actions speak louder than words" saying may be, in certain contexts, it can feel like you're playing a game of charades with a group of people who have never heard of charades. In other words, it can be challenging to convey the message solely through actions, and sometimes you need to provide additional context.

Sharing the progress, current status, and upcoming work of a research project provides cross-functional partners with visibility into the work and an opportunity to collaborate effectively. This can lead to more productive and successful outcomes, as everyone is on the same page and working toward the same goals. So don't be afraid to share the details and bring everyone up to speed. It's like giving them the cheat codes to win the game together!

Share the Research Roadmap—Early and Often

This advice might be limited to researchers embedded in the product teams since they are involved in long-term product strategy.

A research roadmap is a plan created by researchers that outlines the upcoming projects the research team will tackle. It is informed by product roadmaps and research visions and includes timelines and projected impact for each project. The roadmap serves as a guide for the team to prioritize and plan their research efforts in the months ahead.

SAMPLE RESEARCH ROADMAP

Project	Research Question	Timeline	Stakeholder	Study Type	Project Impact
Above the Line					
Language Selection	Usability issues around language selection flow	Q1	PM - Samantha	Usability Study	High
Checkout	Pain Points when checking out	Q2	PM - Ben	Foundational Study	High
Lorem Ipsum	Main Research Question	Q2	PM - Ben	Concept Testing	Medium
Lorem Ipsum	Main Research Question	Q3	Primary Contact	Usability Study	High
Payment	Fears and Concerns when using different payment methods	Q4	Design - Sam	Foundational Study	Medium
Deprioritized (Below the Line)					
Lorem Ipsum	Main Research Question	Q1	Primary Contact	Lorem Ipsum	Medium
Lorem Ipsum	Main Research Question	Q2	Primary Contact	Lorem Ipsum	Low
Lorem Ipsum	Main Research Question	Q3	Primary Contact	Lorem Ipsum	Medium
Lorem Ipsum	Main Research Question	Q4	Primary Contact	Lorem Ipsum	High

Once the research roadmap is ready, share it with your cross-functional partners. Share it on many forums and with multiple teams—the immediate product team, the leadership, the adjacent product teams (where there is work overlap), and researchers across the organization. This helps provide visibility into your upcoming work, providing an opportunity for cross-functional partners and other researchers to reach out to you proactively to collaborate and share timelines that might be critical to know.

Additionally, sharing the research roadmap should not be a one-time activity. Don't assume your product partners remember the research roadmap set three months ago.

"Frankly, I don't remember why I called this meeting."

A quarterly check-in on the progress made and what is upcoming with product and design partners helps ensure that the research roadmap is still aligned with the product roadmap. (*Read more on research roadmaps in Chapter 5.*)

Share Research Plans—To Get Buy-In and Have a Shared Goal

When you are ready to start working on a study actively, regularly share the study updates with the team.

Sometimes you gotta give the people a little sneak peek before you drop the beat. It's like a movie trailer for your actions. You gotta get people excited and leave them wanting more. So, get the hype train rolling!

A research plan is a document that outlines the objectives, goals, and strategies for the research project. It typically includes the research questions or hypotheses, the research design and methodology, the timeline for the project, and the expected outcomes or results. It helps to ensure that the project stays on track and achieves its goals.

Start with sharing the high-level research plan so that cross-functional partners know the research questions and timelines. Regular updates also allow them to provide input and collaborate effectively. When ready, share the study script and the schedule so that cross-functional partners can observe live sessions and hear directly from participants.

You might be wondering that in earlier chapters, we discussed collaboration and involving cross-functional partners in the entire process. And if they are involved in the entire process, why overshare?

Because no matter how well-intentioned your cross-functional partners are, they may often be unable to participate as intently as we would like.

Regularly sharing updates on research projects helps to keep the project at the forefront of everyone's minds, ensuring that they don't forget about it or lose interest over time. Additionally, it provides an opportunity for cross-functional partners to offer feedback and comments asynchronously without needing to schedule a specific meeting or call.

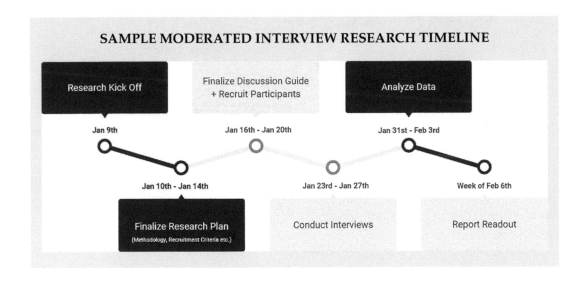

TOM SATWICZ, VP OF RESEARCH, BLINK UX

It's not unusual for people who have been minimally involved in a project to attend a research findings presentation. In many cases, their participation can work well. They're at least familiar with the overall approach and objectives, know the researchers involved, and understand how to make the most out of the research. In other scenarios, these attendees hold weighty perspectives that can be the difference between your study having a wide-ranging impact or quickly being dismissed as irrelevant. How you leverage that knowledge and make use of your stakeholders can flip the value of the work pretty quickly.

For example, Blink UX once presented to a group of stakeholders after completing a study on a non-functioning prototype hardware device. While our researcher presented the results, an industrial designer spoke up with pointed questions about how the sessions were conducted. *What were the participants told about the device and how it would work? Were they shown what would happen if the device was held incorrectly?* His concern was that the findings did not reflect what would happen in the real world—a concern that could be easily misunderstood and echoed across the organization. My takeaway from this experience: ensure that your stakeholders are given the opportunity to review session guides, sessions, and even pilots. Give them the opportunity early on to raise concerns and agree on the best goals for the study.

QUICK TIPS

- Don't just *invite* stakeholders to view your pilot sessions, but *entice* them to come. If you are hosting in-person sessions, snack trays and coffee in the observation room can make it a welcoming place.

- When inviting them, emphasize the importance of their feedback for the success of the project. Two critical parts of a research study are recruiting the right people and asking the right questions. Pilot sessions are a final check that you are asking the right questions.

- Send out an invite for a debrief session at the same time you send an invite for the pilot session. This will make it clear that you are looking forward to their input.

- Give your stakeholders a list of things to look out for in the session. *Are we covering all of our primary objectives? What did we cover in the session that is not crucial? Have we introduced the design, product, concept, etc. in a realistic way?*

SAMPLE RESEARCH PLAN

GOAL

Why is this study important, and what decisions will be made?

STAKEHOLDERS

Who are your points of contact for this project? Names of PM, designer, data scientist, engineer, and content designer involved in this work.

RESEARCH QUESTIONS

What key questions would you like answered by this work?

HYPOTHESES

Do you have any hypotheses as a starting point for further investigation?

ANTICIPATED IMPACT

What impact do you expect to see as a result of this study?

PREVIOUS RESEARCH

Is there any past internal or external research related to this topic area?

METHODOLOGY

Which research methods are most appropriate to answer the research questions? How long will the study be, and what tool will be used?

RECRUITMENT CRITERIA

How many and what kind of participants are best suited for the study?

SCREENER QUESTIONS

What questions will you include in the screener?

STIMULI USED (IF ANY)

What kind of prototypes will be tested? What device—phone, tablet, or computer—would be used?

TIMELINE

When will you finalize the research script, start recruitment, run sessions/field survey, analyze data, and present results?

Provide Regular Updates Throughout a Research Project

Providing regular updates is crucial for keeping stakeholders informed and engaged with the research process. It helps to build trust and credibility by demonstrating progress and transparency. Regular updates also provide an opportunity for stakeholders to provide feedback and insights, which can be incorporated into the research design and execution. Additionally, it keeps stakeholders invested in the research, and they are more likely to utilize the findings in their decision-making processes.

Study Updates: Sharing the study plan a day prior to moderating sessions or fielding the survey refreshes the team's memory around timelines. This also helps nudge members, who are not collaborating on a day-to-day basis, that the research is happening.

SAMPLE MESSAGE ON THE UPCOMING STUDY

Hi team,

Research Study: Language Change Usability Study

A reminder: We are moderating research sessions this week in our West Campus UX Labs. If you would like an invite to observe the sessions, please ping me, and I will send you the details. Here is the *link* to the time and session details.

Here is the **research plan:** *Link*

Research presentation is scheduled for May 29 at 11:00 am

Best,

[Name] UX researcher

Session takeaways: In addition to the final report, in-the-moment updates can also have a significant impact. These updates can be delivered in three ways:

- High-level insights at the end of each session → This approach involves summarizing the key insights gained after every session is completed.
- High-level insights at the end of the day → This approach entails summarizing the key insights gained at the end of each day's research activities.
- High-level insights at the end of the study → This approach involves summarizing the key insights gained after data collection is complete.

Depending on the team's involvement and your bandwidth, either of the above could work well. These real-time updates enable the team to provide feedback to the researcher and make adjustments throughout the research process.

Newsletter: After sharing research schedules and reports on a regular basis, we often don't feel the necessity to share the same information again. However, monthly newsletters or some kind of all-up updates provide visibility on ongoing and completed projects. It also provides an opportunity for cross-functional partners to read reports they might have missed earlier. Lastly, it is a great tool for leadership to get a quick overview of insights. One can summarize multiple studies into one, or if there is already a product newsletter, you can ask your product partners to add the study snippets to their share-out.

If you are an external vendor supporting a project, implementing this strategy may be challenging. However, sharing an executive summary of all studies you have conducted, along with some external research, can be an excellent way to highlight the insights.

Despite newsletters being a useful tool for sharing important updates and insights, let's face it; they can be dense and easily overlooked. That's why it's crucial to get feedback from your audience to ensure your newsletter is hitting the mark. As part of my role, I prioritize seeking feedback from my cross-functional partners during our 1:1 meetings. I want to know if they are finding value in the content and format and if there are any areas where we can improve to make it more engaging and beneficial for them. Ensure your newsletter is something that people look forward to reading and is not just another email in their inbox!

SAMPLE UX RESEARCH NEWSLETTER

The UX research team will provide a monthly update to highlight what we've been doing in the last few months and peek into a few things coming up! We'll publish this at the beginning of each month to help increase transparency, provide visibility into our projects and priorities, and hopefully highlight opportunities for collaboration.

RESEARCH HIGHLIGHT OF THE MONTH

Early this year, we wrapped up a qualitative study focusing on understanding the current and ideal shopping experience on the app. The study highlighted that even though the current shopping experience is fun and provides happiness, the app lacks efficiency and does not help with budgeting. You can find the recent report *here*.

PUBLISHED DECKS TO LOOK OUT FOR

Literature Review on Online Shopping Behavior: As we enter into the discovery phases for our new shopping app, the UX research team summarized the recommendations that should help make decisions on features and use cases that needed to be prioritized for our app. *[Published report here]*

App Checkout Flow Improvements: Participants captured their experience of the checkout flow on the app during in-person lab interviews. The study highlighted that (1) a lack of clarity around pricing and tips undermined users' confidence in their payments and (2) the latency between clicking finish and the confirmation screen, though perceptible, was not a significant detractor *[published report here]*.

UPCOMING STUDIES TO WATCH OUT FOR

Notifications Study: The objective of this study is to assess the usability of notification features before they launch. We will revisit the usability and user experience of key notifications features on the app, cover new scenarios that are not supported, and identify outstanding usability issues as they stand in the latest state of the build *[research plan here]*.

Shopping App Longitudinal Study: The goal of the study is to understand the end-to-end user experience delivered by the shopping app from both usability and product satisfaction perspectives and identify new features that will provide more value to users *[research plan here]*

THE RESEARCH TEAM UPDATE

We have Will Smith, who joined the research team recently to support our checkout workstream. Welcome, Will!

Samantha Taylor, assistant researcher supporting search, is heading out on parental leave. We wish her all the best and can't wait for her to be back.

** We'd love to know if you find this helpful—any feedback is welcome.

Share Research Reports—With One and All

Once you have completed the study, share the research report not only within the immediate team but also broadly. Schedule report readouts and share the deck/document with the immediate product team, the leadership, the adjacent product teams, and researchers across the organization. It is also beneficial to record the report readout sessions and share the recording broadly.

Right Place, Right Time: Similar to the research roadmap, sharing the research report is not a one-time activity. After you have shared with the team, there are many opportunities where surfacing the insights is valuable for the team, especially if it is foundational research. We often assume that the team must remember the research from earlier, but that is rarely the case. Do not rely on the team member's memory and proactively highlight research wherever relevant.

Once upon a time,

I was an embedded researcher on a project where my coworker and I spent 8 months on a 0–1 product launch. It was a challenging experience, but we persevered, and the team finally launched the product. However, it wasn't long before the team started brainstorming ideas for v2.

As we watched the team dive headfirst into a new round of ideation without leveraging past research, my research colleague and I couldn't help but feel frustrated. After all, we had stacks upon stacks of research data, and it seemed like our hard work was being completely disregarded. Remembering how much our partners valued research and had incorporated it in all stages of the v1 launch, we realized that all we needed to do was gently nudge them toward using our existing research.

My colleague and I quickly got to work, creating a summary deck of the research data from the past launch that could serve as thought starters for v2. We presented it to the team, and the reaction was amazing. They gobbled up the insights with excitement and enthusiasm, realizing they could leverage the data to save time and streamline their efforts.

It was a huge win for everyone involved. We were thrilled to advocate for users, and the team was grateful to have a starting point for v2 that didn't require starting from scratch. They had initially been struggling to come up with fresh ideas, but our research provided a much-needed spark of inspiration. It was a reminder that research isn't just a one-time activity but an ongoing process that can continue to add value.

Craft Compelling Research Reports and Presentations

Don't deliver long, rambling reports that don't frame the findings in an actionable way. Communicate your user research findings effectively and concisely.

Long, drawn-out reports will leave your cross-functional partners wondering if they accidentally stumbled into a lecture on quantum physics. Frame them in an actionable way that even partners not working on the product can understand. It is critical to provide them with a concise report that they can read from start to finish without feeling overwhelmed or bogged down by unnecessary details. Remember, we are not trying to win a prize here—you're trying to make an impact and get stuff done!

Be Effective and Clear

When writing a research report, it's critical to remember that the report is not for you. It's for your cross-functional partners, the leadership, and other researchers. Furthermore, research reports have the potential to be reused and reviewed for months or even years after they were written. Make it easy for product and design partners to dive deep into the details of your study if they want to—but don't make it a requirement.

Think about your audience. Think about someone who was not present when the research happened but showed up during the readout or stumbled upon the research link out of curiosity and has no context.

Essentially, I am asking you to be detailed and concise at the same time.

Is that even possible?

To solve for the varied audience who might read your report and the varied amount of information they desire—more detailed to concise—provide high-level information on the objective of the research, the methodology used, and the participant profile, and leverage the appendix by including the discussion guide, survey questionnaire, screener questions, and detailed design flows so that anyone interested in finding the details can access them.

Treat your appendix like a magic box that contains each and every detail related to the study. Include a variety of materials that support the main body of the research study. The appendix can also include raw data, survey responses, interview transcripts, or other primary source materials that were collected during the research process.

By including detailed descriptions of the methodology, data collection procedures, and statistical analyses, future researchers can use the appendix to be inspired by the study.

TOM SATWICZ, VP OF RESEARCH, BLINK UX

TREAT YOUR STAKEHOLDERS LIKE USERS OF YOUR WORK

When presenting to your cross-functional partners and broader audiences, it's important to ensure you ease them into the work at the right level. Imagine that some attendees have no idea what it's about or even what UX research is—someone put the meeting on their calendar and told them they should be there. A quick overview of your study and why you did it can go a long way toward helping them take something impactful from the presentation.

There was a particular client who I worked with over the years, and we conducted several research studies together. Over time, we developed a trusted partnership with a core group of stakeholders. After a particularly large and important study, they extended the final presentation to a broader group. We were excited and ready to share what we had learned across their organization, so excited that we forgot to reset the conversation and step back to UX research 101. We dove right into the findings and were immediately met with confusion and skepticism. *How can you make those claims? Did you conduct a survey?* Instead of sharing what we had learned about their users, we spent the majority of the meeting digging ourselves out of a hole and regaining their trust. In retrospect, when we saw a new set of faces, we should have been careful to explain our approach and what they could learn from it at a high level before diving deep into the findings.

QUICK TIPS

- Have one to two sentences ready to explain what a UX researcher is and what your job includes. *Hello, I'm a UX researcher. My job is to talk with our users and understand how they think about and use our product so that we can create better solutions for them.*

- Emphasize what the research approach is good for and what they can expect to learn. All research has limitations; focusing on that too early in the conversation will undercut the work you want to share. *We observed ten people using our product. This is a great sample size for identifying most of the issues that our users are likely to encounter, understanding why those issues are occurring, and determining the severity of those issues.*

- Include a methods slide to help them gain confidence in your expertise, but don't bore them with stuff only researchers care about. You can always include more details in an appendix for those that want to dive deeper.

Be Comprehensive

Sharing your findings is only a part of the assignment. The audience also needs to listen and *remember*. And the audience often has a short attention span. Being succinct but comprehensive can help your audience process and retain the information more effectively.

Be consistent and make the deck quick to read. The title of your slide should be a takeaway—the most critical takeaway of that slide.

Compare creating slide titles to writing headlines for a gossip magazine—you need to grab people's attention with the juiciest takeaway from that slide. And just like how people skim through magazines, your audience will skim through your slides. So, make sure that even if they only read the titles, they'll be able to understand what you're talking about!

Tip—Once I finish my deck, I always do a run-through by only reading the titles of each slide to ensure that the story gets across.

SLIDE TITLE: Should we limit the choices or provide all options to users?

- Lorem Ipsum I
- Lorem Ipsum II

SLIDE TITLE: Consumers are overwhelmed with too many choices and crave a limited set of options

- Lorem Ipsum I
- Lorem Ipsum II

Create Action Titles. The title should be a key takeaway or 'so what' so that, if time constrained, the audience can only read the title and still get the main message

SEAN RYAN, SR. UX RESEARCHER, GOOGLE

Early in my career, I fell into the habit of writing lengthy book reports. I didn't really have strong narratives in my research. Everything was data! And this showed up in busy slide decks where I tried to cram it all into a PowerPoint report deck. This, I think, is the fundamental difference between a beginner researcher that lacks the awareness or confidence to self-edit when forming their analysis/synthesis of the data.

I think at year 3, or so, my manager finally pulled me aside and said: "This is indulgent work," meaning that it was not of great utility or value to the team. I was sort of offended at the time, but I also really respected this manager's opinion when it came to communications. There was no one better than her at the time for really having a strong narrative that got the attention of leadership. I was working with another researcher at the time, and we ended up going back to the wall to see how we could restructure the report and make it more usable for the team. Ultimately, my research partner had a great idea to synthesize our loose observations into a book of problem statements for the research team, which was much more useful and spoke the language that product teams understood.

As I progressed in my career, I figured out that I was not really helping the product team with this approach to reporting my research findings. The deliverables needed to be strong and crisp, and while there might have been a lot of interesting findings in there, they were lost in a very verbose report deck that lacked a strong central narrative.

My key takeaways from this experience were:

- Work on editing your research findings (what is the elevator pitch or "radio cut," as they say in journalism). Become self-aware enough to be able to self-edit when needed. Nobody has time for a 50+ slide deck.
- Research that doesn't have a strong focus may begin to include too much information, which could become overwhelming and only interesting to the researchers involved.
- Early in your career or in a new job role especially, don't be afraid to take the advice or guidance of a good manager or colleague that might help you with your narrative. Sometimes, as researchers, we become too close to the work and need that point of inflection.

Share a Clear Executive Summary: Provide a succinct summary of the findings. This takes skill and a non-biased attitude. We are often tempted to consider every insight as "very critical," which may not be the case. Think diligently and try to parse "must know insights" from "nice to know." Challenge yourself to only pick five out of many that you must share. The rest can go in the appendix.

The appendix is like the Mary Poppins bag of your research report—you can stuff all the odds and ends that didn't quite make the "Top 5" list into this magical space. And just like Mary Poppins, it can seem like a bottomless pit of wonders and surprises, and a bunch of papers and graphs that someone is sure to read.

Offer Actionable Recommendations

Early in my career, I used to feel overwhelming excitement when presenting my research findings. I was convinced that I had stumbled upon insights that my team had not yet considered and that would prove to be essential to our product strategy. Unfortunately, my enthusiasm did not always yield the reaction I had hoped for.

Reason? My product partners often struggled to figure out how to transform my insights into actionable product recommendations. Over time, I came to realize that merely presenting my findings was insufficient. I needed to make sure that my recommendations were truly impactful and could be easily implemented.

Research decks and documents often miss "why" and "so what." Conveying the insight is critical, but the researcher must also provide a point of view on what action the team can take. Clearly call out recommended actions and owners wherever possible so that when you finish presenting the report, cross-functional partners clearly understand what steps they need to take based on the insights.

An actionable report provides clear recommendations and next steps for product decisions, specific design solutions, and future research needs. It is not prescriptive but rather provides the team with the next possible direction.

Recommendation: Make changes to the CTA design	**Recommendation:** Explore more options for the CTA to look clickable	**Recommendation:** Make the CTA black and 2x2 in size
Too Generic - what kind of changes?	Just Enough	Too Prescriptive

ILANA MEIR, STAFF CONVERSATION DESIGNER, META

When you ask your phone, smart speaker, or any other tech to "Play music," there's a designer behind what happens next. I'm one of those *conversation designers* who specialize in interactions involving voice. In my career, I've designed a wide range of products ranging from automated phone calls to novel augmented reality experiences, and, throughout, incorporating insight into customers' motivations, behaviors, and attitudes has been a crucial component to creating successful products.

As a designer, I'm tasked with answering "What should we make for our customers?" My first question is, "What do they like?" As opposed to intuition, research gives me concrete data that spans the most relevant customer base with a carefully chosen representative sample: I'm no longer designing a product to match the needs of select past customers that I remember but rather our current customers. To create a strong throughline from research to design, there are a few things I look for in a UX research study:

CONTAINS *ACTIONABLE* INSIGHTS

Humans are fascinating. Personally, there's so much I want to know about people's whys and hows out of pure curiosity. But when it comes to work, I put on a filter and scan for information I can turn into an action item. In fact, I will sit with research findings and write my "to-do" in the margins next to every single insight. As you synthesize your research, I recommend thinking about your design partner going through this exercise. Ask yourself for every insight whether your designer could create a clear "to-do" item. This check works particularly well for evaluative studies but works for exploratory ones, too.

Especially if collaborating with designers is new for you, I also recommend spending time getting to know how your design team approaches problems. That way, you can more easily discern what types of insights will be most actionable for them.

DOCUMENTED IN AN ORGANIZED WAY AND CATALOGED WITH OTHER STUDIES IN A LOGICAL, SEARCHABLE PLACE

I'll often refer back to research throughout the product development process. When my team has to make hard trade-offs for the sake of technical feasibility or time, I often return to our values and *our customers' values* to ground our decisions. When the product is complex and requires years to bring to market, being able to quickly find a research study that was conducted a while ago, perhaps even before I even joined the project, is invaluable. I suggest thinking through a documentation and storage strategy to ensure your insights are enduring and that design can reference them all the way through to the product launch.

ANSWERS MY QUESTIONS AND OPENS MY EYES TO NEW CONSIDERATIONS

Before starting to design, I'll have a few questions on my mind already. Good research studies answer these questions. The best studies give me information on topics I never thought to ask that then become central considerations for the product. You may have read this tip before, but it's always been beneficial to involve me early in the research process. When researchers start our conversations before the study, they ensure they're answering my questions, especially if I have a chance to review the protocol to see if there are any specific topics or lines of inquiry I'd like to incorporate. The bonus benefit of having conversations early is researchers get to know what sort of information I'm looking for, and that's when I later get the insights I didn't even know I needed.

Enrich the Narrative by Integrating User Quotes

Including participant quotes in a research report can add significant value by humanizing the research and making it more relatable to the audience. When reading a report with quotes from users, readers can empathize with the users' experiences and connect with their emotions and pain points. This can make the research more impactful and help readers to understand the users' perspective in a more meaningful way.

Moreover, using participant quotes in research reports highlights the fact that the insight is coming from the users and not the researcher, adding credibility to the research findings. It shows that the researcher has taken the time to understand and appreciate the users' experiences, which can build trust with the audience.

However, it's essential to use quotes strategically and not overuse them. Using too many quotes can lead to information overload and make it difficult to understand the key insights. Instead, it's essential to select a few of the best quotes that represent the most critical insights and highlight them in the report.

SAMPLE USER QUOTE

"I don't see any examples where I can look for more details... to understand what this course is about"

" I am confused because it says developer again. I just clicked on developer so I don't' know why I have to click again"

KAM KASHMIRI, VP OF DESIGN, AMAZON PRIME VIDEO

As a design leader, I have always advocated for the integration of UX research and design—the act of learning and developing together—to build empathy, develop a deeper understanding of customers' needs, and design solutions rooted in valuable insights based on those learning. I always advocate for qualitative diary studies, ride-along in people's homes, and similar techniques that are so impactful for researchers and designers to do these together. In fact, I encourage everyone involved, including senior stakeholders, to actively participate and gain firsthand experience. This allows them to develop a profound understanding of how users engage with and perceive our product.

> *Learning together, feeling together, and codeveloping together are critical to frame opportunity areas that benefit the users.*

However, in the absence of immersive research, because that's hard to do sometimes, it's all about storytelling. The research readout should be a journey of learning that takes the audience on a compelling narrative, drawing them into the user's world and showing them the impact of their actions. It should take you from the inception of the hypothesis to its execution. By weaving these qualitative insights into the data, researchers should add depth and meaning and help stakeholders overcome the bias of data.

Speaking tactically, the narration should bridge the gap between the initial problem statement, what insights we gathered related to it, answer the "so what," and provide clarity on the next steps. It should not just accept the challenge but reframe it and look at the broader opportunities we can impact through our work.

One effective technique for storytelling is leveraging the power of films. It distills a 20-page report into a narrative you need everybody in the room to walk away with, understand, and align on. By making films, using customer stories and anecdotes from real customer insights, everybody understands where we started, what we learned, how people felt, and what we will take from this and move forward, and it's much more effective.

In summary, the recipe for success involves everyone deeply involved in the research process, identifying the true user problem (beyond perceived issues), great storytelling, and marrying it with a real conviction about how you move forward.

Keep Them Honest About Research Limitations and How to Interpret Insights

Both qualitative and quantitative research has their limitations, and highlighting them in the research report helps the team make informed decisions. For example, if you are using usertesting.com for unmoderated studies, the participants are usually on the above-average side of being tech-savvy since they are adept at using computers, making accounts, and recording videos. This also holds true for surveys where the survey respondents might be more tech-savvy, given that most surveys are web-based and require some proficiency in using computers and filling out online forms.

Similarly, when interpreting insights, it is critical to consider that observed issues are not scalable to the general population (i.e., just because two out of ten participants experienced a problem does not mean 20% of our customer base will experience the same problem).

Not to forget, we are paying people to concentrate and give us their full attention. They may not be as focused and attentive in the real world, so their observed performance may be higher or lower than normal.

Highlighting the limitations of both qualitative and quantitative research in the research report is essential to ensure that the team can make informed decisions based on the research data. It's crucial to consider the representativeness of the research participants, the scalability of observed issues, and the limitations of observed performance when interpreting research insights.

ANNE MAMAGHANI, RESEARCH STRATEGIST, FOUNDER OF WISDOM DRIVEN UX

COMMUNICATE EFFECTIVELY WITH EXECUTIVES TO ACHIEVE MORE HUMAN-CENTERED PRODUCTS

What does the thought of communicating with executives brings up in many researchers? For many UX Researchers, the experience of trying to get through to executives and other corporate decision-makers is fraught with anxiety. Often, this angst doesn't fully fade over time—even more senior researchers often experience it.

And it's with good reason. Executives often seem to miss, overlook, or even disregard the human-centered solutions whose benefits are so obvious to us researchers. Our passion for creating the best, most useful products for users often seems to run afoul of executive desires.

But we have to communicate our insights, recommendations, and ideas to executives. Without that, we lose critical influence in creating more human-centered products, neglecting the primary responsibility of our UX researcher role.

So we communicate with executives as best we can. This often results in the following ineffective pattern.

THE TYPICAL INEFFECTIVE PATTERN OF COMMUNICATING WITH EXECUTIVES

The researcher, enthusiastic about user-centered approaches and excited to ensure the highest usability of their product(s), sets about doing their job: Collecting user data, analyzing it, synthesizing it, then creating and reporting the resulting insights, recommendations, and ideas.

The researcher may report these directly to an executive, or there may be human or technological intermediaries involved in the communication.

But the executive doesn't necessarily buy into the insights, recommendations, and ideas and instead makes a decision that the researcher considers bad for users. The researcher becomes frustrated and tries different tactics—perhaps trying to educate the executive on the value of user-centered decision-making or trying to demonstrate the product's problems.

Often these tactics don't lead to effective change, and the researcher becomes increasingly angry and perhaps eventually disillusioned with the executive's lack of user-centered decision-making.

Does this sound familiar? If you've been a researcher for a while, you've likely experienced this cycle, observed it, or both, and likely many times. This experience repeats itself in all kinds of organizations every day.

Luckily, there's a way out of this woeful cycle and into effective researcher–executive communication. The rest of this section discusses some actions researchers can take to enable this strong communication.

FIRST, FIND OUT THE ANSWER TO THIS SIMPLE QUESTION

It can be easy to overemphasize what we want executives to understand about our insights, recommendations, and ideas. But the first step is making sure we understand what's important to executives.

If you want executives to value and act on your insights, recommendations, and ideas, then you need to make it clear how those insights, recommendations, and ideas help with what the executive cares about.

To do this, it's important to listen. What is this executive talking about in the organization? What are their goals for the quarter and the year? What KPIs (key performance indicators) are they endorsing? If it's not clear to you, find out. A few ways to do this are asking your manager and other leaders, listening carefully when the executive speaks, and perhaps even asking the executive directly, if necessary.

IT'S USUALLY ABOUT ONE THING

Chances are, the answers to these questions have a direct line to making money for the company. It's likely clear how the executive's focus generates revenue.

A few common examples are improved engagement with the product, increased sales, and reduced costs. Each of these has a direct impact on company revenue.

NEXT, TRANSLATE AND DELIVER

Now that you know what goal is keeping this executive up at night, it's time to demonstrate how your insights, recommendations, and ideas contribute to achieving that goal. (That is, if they do contribute to achieving that goal. If they don't, it will be important to start designing research projects that do clearly contribute to achieving the goal).

Ensure the correlation between your insights/recommendations/ideas and the executive's goal is communicated very directly, clearly, and crisply. It does not require anyone else to make the connection for themselves—make sure it's very clear to see.

Here are some helpful tactics for this direct, clear, crisp communication with executives. Every organization is different, so it's important to assess these and try those that are most likely to be effective in your organization. And, of course, look for those tactics that will work in your organization that are not listed here.

Tactics for Effective Communication With Executives

General	Report-Specific
Listen, listen, listen	Be sure the "so what?" is very clear
Set up 1:1 time with the executive and use this time to understand what their goals are as well as any specific research questions they may have	Find the format that works for the executive and use it, but don't be afraid to experiment: Memes, video clip reels, and other formats can be effective
Design research that answers the key research questions and furthers the executive's goals	Summarize your insights, leaving method and other details available but not leading with those
Deliver insights fast, using discount research methods if you have to	Triangulate qualitative and quantitative data as much as possible
Update the executive about the progress toward your part of their goal	Make recommendations as much as possible

NOW, DO IT

Now that you have a renewed focus on the importance of understanding and delivering on executive goals, go ahead and get started.

It will likely take time to build strong communication. That's OK. Keep diligently listening and persistently trying.

It's worth it to develop effective communication and strong relationships with the executives you work with.

Make It Easy for Team Members to Find Insights They Care About

To empower each team member with the knowledge they need, it's essential to ensure that uncovering valuable insights is a breeze rather than making it feel like finding a needle in a haystack.

Cross-functional partners seek shortcuts and often want to skip to the insights that impact them. They are just trying to be more efficient. When research insights are dense, it can make it hard for our cross-functional partners to look for relevant content and may force them to move on without fully leveraging the recommendations. An effective research report should contain insights that cater to the entire team while also highlighting some insights intended for specific audiences. For instance, a recommendation for a design overhaul might be more relevant to the designer than the data analyst.

By acknowledging each member's unique role and expertise, you can create a research report that maximizes its impact and value for the whole team.

But how do we do this? By drawing their attention to the right insights and customizing the report. For maximum efficiency and impact, we need to narrow the range—or personalize it—for each stakeholder.

Personalize the Reports—Don't Replicate the Same Narration for All

Once a research study is complete, it's crucial to recognize that different cross-functional partners have different needs and interests in the findings. Product managers, for instance, may seek insights to inform changes in strategy, while designers may want to know about potential interface improvements. Data scientists may be interested in complementary data trends, and engineers may need to be aware of potential edge cases.

To address these varied needs, it's helpful to schedule a team readout to present the research findings to the entire cross-functional team. However, it's also essential to conduct individual readouts with each partner, focusing on the specific findings that matter to them.

This approach provides several benefits:

- It ensures that each cross-functional partner receives tailored information relevant to their role and responsibilities. This helps to increase their engagement and enables them to contribute meaningfully to the research.
- This approach allows cross-functional partners to ask more targeted questions, which can further deepen their understanding of the findings.
- These discussions help us gain insight into our cross-functional partner's thoughts and perspectives, facilitating more in-depth discussions around a set of insights.
- It allows researchers to seek explanations for insights that may not be relevant to our product or design partners and uncover any underlying reasons behind their disinterest.

Strategically Tag Cross-Functional Partners in Research Documents

To improve the visibility and engagement of cross-functional partners in the research plan and report, it's important to tag them in the appropriate places. This involves identifying the specific slides or sections where their input or expertise is needed and directing their attention to those areas.

For instance, if you require your designer to take notice of a specific user interface (UI) element, tag them in that slide to draw their attention. If you want your data analyst to provide additional statistics to support qualitative insights, guide their focus to the relevant insights.

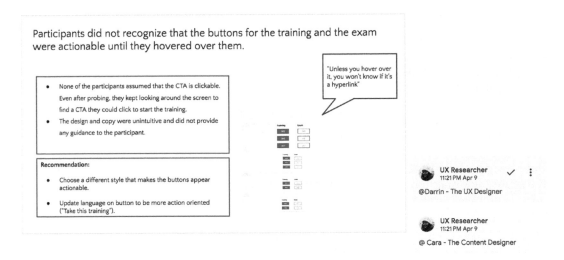

By tagging cross-functional partners in this way, you not only enhance their involvement in the research but also facilitate their ability to contribute meaningfully. This approach also helps to streamline the feedback process and ensures that each partner's input is integrated into the research seamlessly.

Timestamp and Label Video Recordings of Research Sessions

Often, I spice up my research reports by adding a voiceover. This allows product partners to consume the content at their own convenience, which is particularly handy in today's world of remote work and global time zones.

But to enhance the accessibility and usability of video recordings of research sessions, I tag the cross-functional partners with timestamps. This involves adding timestamps and labels to important sections of the video to help cross-functional partners navigate and understand the content easily.

Timestamping and labeling the video recordings of research sessions not only makes it easy for cross-functional partners to follow along but also enables them to refer back to specific sections as needed. This approach helps to improve collaboration and ensure that all partners have a clear understanding of the research findings and implications.

1:20 @John (PM)—Pain point around checkout flow
3:14 @Samantha (Eng)—Edge Case
2:25 @Rohan (Design)—Usability Feedback

Acknowledge the Contribution of Team Members

How do you feel when your PMs recognize your contribution? You feel valued, right? This is a universal feeling.

While researchers may lead the end-to-end research process, a successful study requires a collaborative effort. If your cross-functional partners proactively contribute to the research by offering insights, contributing to research questions, and making time to observe live sessions or review designs ahead of schedule, it's important to acknowledge their efforts.

By recognizing their contributions, you foster a culture of collaboration and encourage your partners to continue actively engaging in the research process. Moreover, acknowledging your cross-functional partners' efforts demonstrates that you value their input and are invested in their success.

It's crucial to take the time to express gratitude and acknowledge them.

Here are a few effective ways to acknowledge the contributions of your cross-functional partners:

- *Add their names to the report*: If your report is a document, you can add the names of your cross-functional partners at the end of the document, acknowledging their contributions and sharing credit for their input.
- *Tag the communication thread*: If you're using a communication platform like Slack or Teams, you can tag the thread where you shared your report and acknowledge the contributions of your cross-functional partners.
- *Use the introduction or last slide in the presentation*: If you're using a Google Deck or any other presentation platform, consider using the introduction or last slide to highlight the outstanding contributions of your cross-functional partners.

SAMPLE ACKNOWLEDGMENT

APPENDIX B: CORE TEAM

- Sonal Srivastava, UX Research
- Darrin Duncan, UX Design
- Cara Cooper, Content Design
- Daniel Davidson, Design Product Manager
- Peter Phillips, Product Manager
- Emma Evans, Engineer

Thank you, @Darrin Duncan, @Cara Cooper, @Daniel Davidson, @Peter Phillips, and @Emma Evans, for playing an integral role in this research by diligently contributing to the research plan and following the observer protocol.

By adopting these simple but effective strategies, you ensure that all stakeholders see your appreciation and recognition of their hard work and dedication to the research process. Your partners feel valued and invested in the process.

Be Proactive and Take the Lead

There may be times when you need to take a more proactive approach to ensure that you have the necessary resources and buy-in from stakeholders.

In some cases, this may require encouraging your cross-functional partners to prioritize research and allocate time for the research process. Achieving this requires clear communication and a willingness to advocate for the importance of research and its impact on product development.

Additionally, it may be necessary to highlight the potential risks and missed opportunities that could result from not prioritizing research. By demonstrating the value of research and its potential impact on the product or organization, you can encourage your cross-functional partners to make room for research and leverage its insights.

Forsee Gaps in User Understanding and Advocate for Research

As researchers, we develop a keen sense of user needs and trends by keeping a close eye on our target audience and our ears to the ground. However, there may be times when our cross-functional partners are not as attuned to these needs and may not see the value in additional research. Conversely, they may view research as a potential disruption to a product launch.

In these situations, it falls on the researcher to generate curiosity and present the case for additional research. This may require showcasing the potential benefits of the research insights and demonstrating how they can positively impact the product or organization.

At the same time, it's important to be efficient in conducting the research, minimizing disruption to the launch timeline and ensuring that the research process is streamlined and effective. This may involve leveraging existing resources and data, using agile research methods, or working closely with cross-functional partners to identify key research questions and goals.

Allow me to illustrate this point with an example from my experience.

I once supported a new product launch, where the entire team was very immersed in research throughout product development. We spent months on foundational research and concept testing and used the insights to design the system. However, there was no room to conduct a usability study since we were soon approaching the launch date. When the almost final designs were ready, there were high-severity usability issues I could foresee, and I strongly advocated for a usability study. It was hard to convince the team as the leadership had already widely announced the system launch, and any delay would look bad.

I was facing questions such as "We know enough and can rely on our intuition now."

Instead of rallying the whole team, I focused my energy on the PM and lead designer. Then I worked on a research plan such that the end-to-end study would take just three days. I also highlighted to the PM and designer that many usability issues we may find might not even require a major overhaul. Minor content and design changes might suffice. Smaller timelines and smaller changes convinced them to go ahead with the research.

I put together the research plan and the discussion guide on day 1. I used an online recruiting tool to recruit participants with a fast turnaround time. The only limitation was that the participant pool was generic. On day 2, I conducted sessions. On day 3, I spent half a day on analysis and presented at the end of the day. Since this was a very short time, I only focused on two things: (1) high-severity red flags that would make the product fail and (2) instead of polishing a deck, I directly used user videos on the high-severity issue to drive home the point.

There was minimal convincing needed after that, and design and content resources were put on the project to prioritize the high-severity issue and fix them ASAP.

Ultimately, by staying attuned to user needs and trends and advocating for additional research when necessary, we can help our product teams stay ahead of the curve and continue to innovate in an ever-changing landscape.

AMELIE WERNER, GLOBAL HEAD OF DESIGN OPERATIONS, UX RESEARCH AND COMMERCE DESIGN, AMAZON PRIME VIDEO

FORWARD-THINKING MINDSET

When I look at what research brings to the mix, I am inspired by how researchers are able to tap into the heart of what truly matters to customers. Creating great user experiences is about bringing things to life. We can't do that without a fundamental understanding of what customers want. Researchers can see what's on the horizon (or around corners in some cases!) and help create meaningful moments for customers around the world. By learning from our customers, we ensure that new and diverse perspectives provide us with insights to build an incredible experience for everyone.

I think of my superpower as being able to align teams against common goals. I can see what's on the horizon and ensure our team is prioritizing and creating work that will make the biggest impact on our customers and business. I strongly advocate for my research teams also to have a forward-thinking mindset, constantly seeking to anticipate what lies ahead. It is crucial for us to collaborate closely with our product and design partners, ensuring that our collective efforts are focused on delivering the most significant impact for our customers and the business as a whole. This approach has proven immensely valuable throughout my career, enabling me to make meaningful contributions and drive success.

When I first joined Amazon Prime Video, there wasn't a UX research team. It was a huge gap not only for the UX team and product partners, but it trickled down into incomplete insights in what we were building for our customers. I advocated for all the myriad reasons why research is so critical and got a small team built. It helped us gather data to make better decisions, test ideas we were thinking through, and build stronger partnerships with our product partners as they started to see how our assumptions could be validated or invalidated by what we were finding. We were able to show the impact and then grow the team. Today that team is a big part of discovering and prioritizing the most important problems Prime Video must solve for its customers.

By keeping a pulse on emerging trends, customer needs, and industry advancements, research helps us steer our product and design teams toward the most promising opportunities and influence key decisions. This proactive approach empowers research teams to go beyond reacting to immediate demands and instead strive to anticipate future challenges and opportunities.

Follow-Up on UX Research Recommendations

Once you wrap up a study, how many research recommendations make it to the product or design roadmap?

Few? Some? None? What about the others?

Even given that not all insights can be implemented, if you find many research recommendations are not being acted upon, leverage your 1:1s with product and design partners to receive concrete feedback on why the insights are deprioritized. Once a study is wrapped and you have a list of insights, work closely with your product and design partners in the decision-making and implementation.

My typical approach is to create an Excel sheet that outlines the research insights and recommendations, and then I ask the team, "Are we currently addressing these issues? If not, why not?" For any areas where the team is not addressing the recommendations, I try to understand whether they plan to address them in the future. If not, I inquire about potential limitations such as privacy, legal, or technological constraints that may be preventing action.

Insights and recommendations that cannot be addressed immediately fall into the "later" category. These items can be incredibly useful in future product roadmap sessions, providing a framework for future development initiatives.

Ultimately, it's essential to not only conduct thorough studies but also ensure that the insights and recommendations are acted upon. By working closely with cross-functional teams and prioritizing actionable insights, researchers can help ensure that their studies have a lasting impact on the product and organization as a whole.

TEMPLATE: UX RESEARCH RECOMMENDATIONS AND RATIONALE FOR NOT IMPLEMENTING

Project Area	Recommendation	Primary Contact	Are we working on it?	If No, Why Not?
Share	Explore more Share Icons	SB	Yes, Now	
	Option to disable sharing	JS	Yes, Later	
	Lorem Ipsum	JS	Yes, Later	
	Lorem Ipsum	SB	Not Sure	Shortage of resources
Commerce	Make the subscription flow concise	RO	No	Technological Limitations
	Lorem Ipsum	RO	No	Legal Concerns
	Lorem Ipsum	TJ	No	Not sure about long term impact
	Lorem Ipsum	TJ	Not Sure	Pending Leadership Approval
Friends and Family	Lorem Ipsum	BB	Not Sure	ROI for business not yet justified

Colead Brainstorms and Design Sprints With Design and Data Analytics

Design sprints are often considered for design only, maybe because they have it in the name?

But what is a good fuel for a design sprint? User-backed data. For the design brainstorm, the goal is to generate many ideas by leveraging the collective thinking of the group, engaging with each other, and building on other ideas. I always recommend starting the sprint by reviewing past research findings and data analytics to get a clear understanding of people's problems and expected outcomes.

To take things further, I recommend and collaborate with my design partners to filter out ideas objectively using a scoring system. One of my favorite methods for this purpose is the RICE methodology, which is highly effective and applies to most design sprints and brainstorming sessions. This approach helps us evaluate ideas based on their potential impact, reach, confidence, and effort required, making it easier to identify and prioritize the most valuable ideas for further development.

RICE (by *Sean McBride*) is a popular prioritization tool where we first estimate how many people each idea will reach. Then we calculate the impact.

$$\frac{\text{Reach x Impact x Confidence}}{\text{Effort}} = \text{RICE Score}$$

The impact is difficult to measure precisely. So, we choose from a multiple-choice scale: 3 for "massive impact," 2 for "high," 1 for "medium," and so on and so forth. Afterward, we determine the confidence level by giving a percentage score delineating the level of confidence regarding the reach and impact. Then we calculate the effort based on the number of resources and time spent on design and engineering. Then we combine them into a single score to compare ideas at a glance.

SARAH SIMPSON, PRODUCT DESIGN MANAGER, META

As a designer, I've worked on several 0 to 1 projects in my career where research was critical to defining our strategic vision for a product space. One specific project that stands out to me is when we were identifying new opportunities that would appeal to a specific audience.

From the start of the project, the researcher played a critical role in defining the brainstorming goal, using trends and market research for the audience as a guide. This helped the team produce a broad range of unique concepts from the start and then narrow in as we gained insights. The researcher recommended using paper prototypes with just two to four key screens to visualize the concept. This made design time faster and ensured participants focused on the core concept and not detailed interactions.

The research report highlighted the key value of each concept, what resonated and what didn't, and provided recommendations on concepts to pursue. From this, the team was able to drop nonviable ideas, iterate on promising ones, bundle concepts together, and generate new concepts for the subsequent sessions.

The researcher's expertise and guidance allowed us to successfully run sprint-style concept testing. This resulted in our team testing at least a dozen concepts within just a few weeks, enabling us to learn (and fail) fast by getting early signals before investing in ideas that weren't actually great opportunities. Their guidance got the team out of internal debates on which direction to pursue based on personal preferences and defined the best research methods to drive the team toward faster outcomes.

In my opinion, I would attribute the success of the project to the researcher's strategic actions:

- She helped structure the initial brainstorm to focus on the audience and opportunity space, resulting in a broader range of unique concepts to test.
- Recommended the level of fidelity that allowed the team to work efficiently within a short timeframe while gaining the right level of insight to make decisions.
- Provided reports with unbiased, collective insights with clear recommendations and opportunity areas, ensuring the team didn't hone in on personal preferences or one-off comments from observing the sessions.

THEO FOLINAS, STAFF UX DESIGNER

During my time at Thumbtack, I was partnered with a very thoughtful and collaborative user researcher named Erik. To me, Erik defined what it meant to be a great user research lead. He understood product prioritization, pushed to get the team insights before any large project started, and was flexible and collaborative. Erik made time to bring in all his cross-functional partners into his research process.

One of the projects we worked on together was a complete redesign of the customer experience. At the time, Thumbtack customers had to submit their project details and wait for professionals to send quotes. We were hearing from users that they wanted to see who these professionals were before submitting any details. A key part of this redesign was to distill the user feedback into key themes. I distinctly remember Erik pulling me and others into a massive room with hundreds of stickies where we all grouped and highlighted insights together. He made it fun and gave everyone the chance to be a part of the process. From there, Erik framed these insights as "how might we (HMW)" and led a cross-functional brainstorm. Being able to clearly see how these prompts connect to real users' problems helps remove assumptions and improve the impact of ideas.

5

Advanced Strategies for Effective Cross-Functional Collaboration

DOI: 10.1201/9781003391036-5

Now, let us shift our focus to some time-intensive strategies that yield the best results when planned on a six-monthly or yearly basis. These strategies involve making significant investments, but the returns they bring are equally substantial. While executing these strategies may pose challenges for those who are not fully integrated into the team, there are aspects of these approaches that can benefit everyone involved.

Within this chapter, we will explore the concept of leadership immersion. We will discuss various ways of organizing immersions, including their frequency, and delve into the process of planning and preparing leaders for the immersion day. Additionally, we will take an in-depth look at the value of research roadmaps. I will talk about why having a research roadmap is valuable, the optimal time to start building one, and outline a collaborative and effective process for developing it. Lastly, I will share some creative tactics for sharing research findings, which can prove highly beneficial in our endeavors.

By taking the time to focus on these strategies, we pave the way for substantial growth and success. Their implementation may require effort, but the rewards they bring will make it all worthwhile.

Lead Leadership Research Immersions

Leadership research immersions are research sessions geared toward leadership that provide a chance for them to hear directly from the users about user pain points, needs, and behaviors.

In certain organizations, this may be referred to as a roadshow or empathy day, which has a similar purpose—providing cross-functional partners with a firsthand experience of user behavior and actions by taking them into the field and fostering greater empathy and understanding of the user perspective among all stakeholders.

Benefits of such immersions include but are not limited to

- Developing more profound empathy for the people we build products and services for
- Gaining an understanding of how we come up with insights that the team should be using to build solutions
- Gleaning research-based insights that spark new ideas and strategies
- Learning to speak the same language as our users
- Developing a better understanding of what the research team does

Are you wondering–How leadership immersions are different from cross-functional partners observing regular research sessions? While not fundamentally dissimilar, these approaches differ in logistic planning and the target audience. The leadership is often unable to carve time to join live sessions scheduled to product timelines. Hence, with research immersion, the researcher prioritizes the time and day when leads can provide focused time and be fully immersed in the experience.

There are multiple ways of organizing research immersion and getting leadership to hear directly from the users. Some of the ways include:

- Visiting users in their homes
- Scheduling live sessions
- Watching a curated video reel

Each of these methods has its own set of advantages and disadvantages, and the best approach will depend on factors such as budget, availability of cross-functional partners, and ease of access to the target audience.

Let's delve into each of these methods in greater detail.

Visiting users in their homes: In-home interviews are lengthy conversations that explore the values, desires, frustrations, and aspirations of users and help to identify discrepancies between what people say they do and what they actually do. Leadership gets to see firsthand what else is happening around users when they use the product in a certain way and how the product/concept fits into their everyday life.

(i) In-home research offers several key advantages, including

1. *Contextual insights*: People's experiences are heavily influenced by their sur-
   roundings, and in-home research provides a unique opportunity to observe
   this. By studying participants in their natural settings, researchers can uncover
   contextual clues that can lead to new avenues for product development.
2. *Discovery of new personas*: Assumptions about users and their behavior can be
   challenged by conducting in-home research. By observing a diverse range of
   people and factors, we discover new personas and gain a better understanding of user needs and preferences.
3. *Action-based insights*: In-home research emphasizes actions over words.
   Survey responses may not always reflect actual behavior, but by observing
   participants in their relaxed and familiar environment, researchers can gain
   a more accurate understanding of how people interact with products and
   services.

For ease of planning, you can either recruit participants from the location where your leadership team is based or, preferably, travel to cities where you can engage with the demo-
graphics that are most relevant to your research topic.

*For one of my immersion sessions, I recruited participants from Modesto, CA, with the intent of
being outside of the tech bubble to conduct sessions with people who use our products. The sessions were in people's homes. This was crucial for understanding users' experiences, pain points,
and attitudes outside of Silicon Valley and was a full-day experience. We debriefed at the office
afterward to discuss what the leads learned from our users and their thoughts on the immersion
experience.*

WHEN LEADERSHIP ASKED, "WHY WATSONVILLE AND NOT A NEARBY PLACE?"

Watsonville is a city in Santa Cruz County just outside of the San Francisco Bay Area. Unlike the Bay Area, the economy of Watsonville centers predominantly around the farming industry. Other leading industries are construction, manufacturing, and other privately owned restaurants in the area.

Here is how Watsonville compares to the Bay Area and beyond and helps us also learn from users who are perhaps different than folks working for tech:

	Watsonville	San Francisco	US median
Median household income	$51,548	$96,265	$57,652
Population that is high school graduate or higher	59.3%	87.9%	87.3%
Population that has broadband internet subscription	71%	84.5%	78.1%
Percentage of population in poverty	15.6%	11.7%	12.3%

Scheduling live (remote or lab) sessions: If traveling is a constraint or organizing in-home interviews is out of budget, you may consider organizing virtual or in-lab interviews where your leadership team can observe the sessions together. Similar to in-home interviews, plan for this ahead of time and ensure your leadership team is available to watch the entire session. Based on the schedule, you can plan for debriefing later in the day or the next day but soon enough so that it is fresh for leadership to share their experiences and learnings.

Watch a curated video reel: If you intend to curate the experience or only have a few hours to engage your leadership, you can plan a 2- to 3-hour session similar to a workshop. Occasionally, it can be challenging to convince leadership to commit to a full-day immersion, and a shorter workshop can be a great compromise to demonstrate value and gain their support.

To ensure that the workshop is effective, you should structure it to include not only insights but also a focus on creating a high-quality video reel. Capture participants' faces and voices clearly and create a highlight reel (*a video that compiles the best clips from all your research sessions*) with the participants' experiences that are most insightful. Ensure to keep the reel long enough to set the context and for cross-functional partners to have rich takeaways. Wrap up with a debrief to discuss the findings, highlight key takeaways, and address any questions or concerns that may arise.

DO'S AND DON'TS FOR CROSS-FUNCTIONAL PARTNERS OR LEADERSHIP TO KEEP IN MIND WHEN OBSERVING SESSIONS:

- *Respondents are the experts of their world*: We value all our respondents equally. They are the experts in how they live their lives, and we are there to listen to their stories and understand their needs and motivations. We should never correct a participant or explain how our products work. Respondents' perceptions, experiences, and feelings are always valid, regardless of how they align with our ideas about how our products work.

- *Capture first-order reality*: Take note of what your participants do and say (first-order reality) rather than your interpretation (second-order reality). Understand the 'why' rather than assuming or layering your interpretations.

- *Observe the respondent's environment and behavior*: What people do is as important as what they say. In addition, people's environments often give us additional insight into their lives and how they use our products. People may say that your product is easy to use, but we may see them struggle to use various features in reality. They may say they love your product, but they may live in places that make it hard to access reliable and fast internet. Remember to write down notes about the context in addition to notes about what participants say.

- *Come with an open mind*: If you're fixed on a certain outcome, you'll selectively read the output in your favor. The point of research is to be humbled by it and be inspired to do better.

- *Do not correct participants or explain how products work*: If participants have an incorrect understanding of how our products work, we do not intervene or correct them. Let the moderators take the lead and navigate the conversation.

- *Flexibility makes for good research*: People don't lead cookie-cutter lives. Be prepared to change your plans depending on your participant's needs. We may spend more or less time with them, depending on the flow of the conversation.

- *Wait for moderators to seek questions from you*: Moderators will take the lead with the discussion but will pause at the end of the key sections to check if you have any questions. Your input is very valuable, but please try to wait for these pause points to ask them so that the researcher can continue with the flow of inquiry in each section.

Frequency: The frequency of immersion sessions can vary depending on the organization's needs and resources. Quarterly immersions that focus on different topics or different leads each time can be effective in keeping leads engaged and up-to-date on customer needs and preferences. However, if you have the same leadership cohort and wish to maintain consistency, six-monthly or yearly immersions can be sufficient.

It's worth noting that the frequency of immersion sessions can also be influenced by the rate of change within the industry or the organization itself. Rapid changes in customer preferences, new competitors entering the market, or significant shifts in the business landscape may require more frequent sessions to ensure that leadership is adequately informed and equipped to make informed decisions.

Regularly evaluating the effectiveness of the sessions and adjusting the frequency accordingly can help ensure that they remain a valuable tool for leadership.

Planning: Immersions are time- and resource-sensitive, especially in-home sessions, and need to be planned meticulously. Small mistakes can cost the executives valuable time and make them less inclined to attend the next time.

I would like to share some tips that have helped me achieve success with immersion sessions:

- *Teamwork*: Having a strong team of researchers and research managers has been the most crucial starting point for me. There is a lot to manage—from logistics to recruitment to constant communication with leads to keep them excited and answer any open questions.
- *Timely updates*: Providing regular updates on the schedule and any change is essential. Keeping everyone accountable for their role helps me keep everything on track and smooth.
- *Evangelizing*: Leveraging my manager to use their 1:1s with leads to evangelize the immersion was valuable. This helped minimize drop-offs, and the leads came to the immersion excited and prepared.
- *Working with executive assistants*: Executive assistants of the leads can be a huge support system throughout, from finding the perfect day and answering any and every question along the way. However, this might not be applicable in every case.
- *Planning early*: Find a time that works for everyone and does not coincide with performance evaluations, product roadmaps, team off-sites, and vacation days. You can do a poll to find the date that works best and block off calendars for three months in advance. You can also keep checking in with the leads to avoid unforeseen circumstances.
- *Creating a research immersion booklet*: I draft a booklet with the most frequently asked questions, such as the protocol for observing and note-taking during sessions, the value of a small sample size in qualitative studies, different methods used in research, and the roles of research at various stages of product development. You can also create prompts for note-taking in the booklet. This helps immensely with the context-setting.
- *Prepping the participants*: For in-home sessions, the participants should be informed beforehand that they will have four to five attendees from the company in their house

and share the names and research profiles with them to make sure they are comfortable and in the know. Similarly, for remote interviews, inform them that a few colleagues would join the call, act as passive observers, and help with note-taking.

- *Having multiple tracks*: For in-home interviews, you might need to split the activity into multiple tracks if you have many leaders attending. Use the same script and a common debrief session to maximize learning but conduct parallel research sessions to avoid overwhelming the participant and give attendees enough room to observe and participate.

- *Having vans with Wi-Fi*: For in-home sessions, I try to rent vehicles with Wi-Fi. This is important for allowing leads to keep up with their responsibilities between sessions and reply to urgent emails and chats.

- *Customized research topic*: Some of the insights, even though alarming, are often out of scope for leads to take action on. On the other hand, they can act immediately on feedback that they have more control over. So, having a more tailored topic of interest might be better. I seek research questions from leadership themselves to ensure we are helping them bridge any gaps they have in their reasoning.

- *Backup recruits*: For both in-home and lab sessions, ensure a backup participant for each session. Any canceled sessions due to participants not showing up are a missed opportunity to show research value.

Prepping Leaders for the Immersion Day

As research immersion may not be standard practice within an organization, it is essential to take the time to prepare the leadership team so that they know what to expect on the day of the immersion.

- Prep the leads before sessions begin: Set aside 30 minutes before starting your first research session to review the research immersion booklet and help answer any questions. You can also use this time to discuss the protocol around taking photos, asking questions during sessions, the rationale behind the location you picked, and in-home versus lab interviews.

- *Discuss key takeaways*: After every session, discuss the key elements from the sessions. You can also have an informal AMA (ask-me-anything), which allows both the leads and researchers an opportunity to share their experiences and how to better partner.

- *Assign roles*: To keep the leads engaged and focused, give each of them a specific role for each session. So, for instance, if one is the primary notetaker, the other is given the role of observing the participant, the environment, the artifacts around, etc.

- If participating in in-home interviews, also share with them that they need to be mindful of the following:
  - Not wearing company-branded clothes: Company-branded clothes can send intentional or unconscious signals to participants and bias their responses. Casual, comfortable clothing is best as we might be sitting on the floor, on the patio, or in the kitchen in houses with or without air-conditioning.
  - *Try not to use laptops and phones during sessions*: Even if you bring your laptop and phone, please don't use them! It is disrespectful to participants!
  - *Bring a notebook and a pen*: Take notes and capture what you observe.

Last but not least, debrief with the leads: After wrapping up the sessions, crave time for a debrief session. This can take multiple forms. The one I enjoy the most is asking each lead to pick a participant and summarize that participant for everyone in the room. They also share one positive story and one challenge the participant faced.

In the end, I also ask them explicitly about the immersion experience to help improve the program for future immersion. Soliciting feedback from the leads helps me identify areas for improvement and inform changes that can increase the effectiveness and value of future immersion sessions.

SAMPLE DEBRIEF TEMPLATE FOR EACH SESSION CAPTURE

Pain Points: A place where the user struggles or was confused. Also, a situation where the user seems disappointed or unsure

Surprises: Something that made you think, challenged an assumption or changed your perspective

Key Takeaways: Big findings that are important for the project

Parking Lot: A Place to put anything that doesn't fit into the above (including questions!)

Pain Points	Surprises
Key Takeaways	**Parking Lot**

FOR OVERALL LEARNING

- What are the major patterns and common themes that emerged in the participant responses?
- How were participants different from each other?
- What stories will help you remember this immersion day (related to what you heard in sessions)?
- What positive stories will you remember?
- What struggles will you remember?

Maximize Your Impact With A Research Roadmap

In the previous chapter, we discussed the importance of sharing research roadmaps frequently and at an early stage. This chapter will delve deeper into what research roadmaps entail, the advantages of creating one, and the steps involved in crafting a comprehensive roadmap.

A research roadmap outlines the different projects that the research team will tackle in the upcoming months. The projects are populated from product roadmaps and highlight topics that will be studied, cross-functional partners involved, the effort required, and timelines.

Research roadmaps are common for researchers embedded in the team, but if you are an outside vendor commissioned to conduct multiple studies, a research roadmap can be a valuable tool for you too.

Why Are Research Roadmaps Valuable?

- *To maintain a balance of headcount and projects*: A research roadmap provides valuable insights into achieving a balanced headcount and project ratio. Offering a clear view of upcoming projects enables research leaders to make informed decisions about the optimal allocation of resources. Whether seeking to increase headcount or reduce project load, the roadmap serves as a valuable tool for building a persuasive case. Ultimately, it empowers research teams to operate more efficiently and achieve greater success.

- *To manage ad hoc research requests*: Managing ad hoc research requests can be challenging and disrupt day-to-day work. To avoid thrash and ensure that research efforts align with business objectives, it is essential to have a research roadmap in place. A research roadmap provides a structured approach to managing oncoming or unexpected research requests, ensuring they are prioritized and aligned with the organization's goals. They also help cross-functional partners understand your priorities if you need to turn down an ad hoc research request.

- *To get early cross-functional buy-in for your research*: A planned research roadmap helps you get buy-in before you do research and keeps cross-functional partners aware of when insights will come.

- *To empower you as a leader*: Taking ownership of a research roadmap positions you as a proactive leader instead of merely being a passive recipient of requests.

- *To promote better collaboration with other researchers*: Research roadmaps enhance collaboration among researchers by providing visibility across teams, enabling them to connect ideas and work together more effectively.

- *To manage work/life balance*: Knowing in advance which weeks are research-heavy and when you can take a break allows you to anticipate and plan for your upcoming weeks, months, and even the next few weeks.

When Is the Best Time to Start Building a Research Roadmap?

The best time to start working on a roadmap is when the product roadmap draft is ready.

Some organizations map the product roadmap a year out in advance, while others opt for shorter three-month cycles. Finally, it also hinges on whether you have been part of the project from day 0 or joined the team or company later on. Either way, you should start early by putting together a roadmap as soon as you learn about the project, team, and company priorities.

Now let's focus on what a collaborative and effective research roadmap process looks like.

Keep a close eye on the product roadmap: The research roadmap needs to align closely with the product roadmap. And to do so, being involved in the product roadmap discussions helps the researcher understand team, project, and leadership priorities. Additionally, it also helps researchers sense where the gaps in understanding user pain points, needs, etc. exist in teams' thinking and what research would be most valuable.

Seek research requests: Once the product roadmap draft is ready, leverage your 1:1s with cross-functional partners to seek research requests. What and when do they anticipate research input being valuable?

Recommend research topics proactively: While you are seeking input from cross-functional partners, in parallel, also note projects (especially foundational in nature) where teams are not seeking help but where you believe that research insights would be valuable.

ⓘ WHAT IS A FOUNDATIONAL VERSUS AN EVALUATIVE STUDY?

Foundational user research is conducted at the beginning of the product development cycle, typically during the ideation or concept stage. The primary goal of foundational research is to understand the needs, behaviors, and attitudes of potential users and customers to inform product strategy and design. Foundational research may include methods such as user interviews, surveys, and observational studies.

Evaluative user research, on the other hand, is conducted after a product has been developed and is closer to release or is already in the market. The primary goal of evaluative research is to assess the usability, effectiveness, and user satisfaction of the product to identify areas for improvement and inform future iterations. Evaluative research may use a combination of qualitative and quantitative methods, such as usability testing, A/B testing, and user surveys.

Draft research roadmap: Once all of the above is complete, compile them into a user-friendly format, such as a spreadsheet or deck, that visually represents all the possible research that could be conducted. In most circumstances, this list is usually bigger than what is realistically possible to study.

DRAFT RESEARCH ROADMAP THAT LISTS ALL PROJECTS

Project	Research Question	Team Priority	Impact	Timeline Q1 = Jan-Mar Q2 = Apr-Jun Q3 = Jul-Sep Q4 = Oct-Dec	Stakeholder
Language Selection	Usability issues around language selection flow	P0 ▾	High	Q1	PM - Samantha
Checkout	Pain Points when checking out	P1 ▾	High	Q2	PM - Ben
Payment	Fears and Concerns when using different payment methods	P1 ▾	Medium	Q4	Design - Sam
Search and Find	JTBD for Search	P2 ▾	Low	Q3	Leadership Ask
Lorem Ipsum	Main Research Question	P1 ▾	Medium	Q2	PM - Ben
Lorem Ipsum	Main Research Question	P0 ▾	High	Q4	Primary Contact
Lorem Ipsum	Main Research Question	P2 ▾	Low	Q2	Primary Contact
Lorem Ipsum	Main Research Question	P1 ▾	Medium	Q3	Primary Contact
Lorem Ipsum	Main Research Question	P0 ▾	Medium	Q1	Primary Contact

Next, Prioritize Projects: Then comes the critical task of prioritization, and collaboration is key here. Once you have populated a list of projects, you need to prioritize projects based on impact, available resources, and level of urgency.

Next, share the list of research topics with key stakeholders such as leadership, managers, and other researchers. These individuals have visibility into the team's priorities and can offer valuable input for project prioritization. It is essential to clarify the expected timeline and dependencies required for each project to ensure a successful outcome.

The output of this prioritization task is a list of the same research projects from earlier but ranked by priority or timeline (Q1 to Q4) and divided by below-the-line and above-the-line items.

Above the line here is defined as projects that you commit to supporting. Below the line are defined as projects that are deprioritized either due to resource constraints or because the team already has sufficient insights or the product or feature is overall a lower priority for the team.

Unless your role is limited to conducting usability studies, ensure your roadmap balances foundational and evaluative studies to provide support across all stages of the product life cycle. Prioritize the right projects that you can complete on time and also help cross-functional partners see how your projects ladder up to the team's roadmap.

FINAL RESEARCH ROADMAP WITH PRIORITIZED PROJECTS

Project	Research Question	Timeline	Stakeholder	Study Type	Project Impact
Above the Line					
Language Selection	Usability issues around language selection flow	Q1	PM - Samantha	Usability Study	High
Checkout	Pain Points when checking out	Q2	PM - Ben	Foundational Study	High
Lorem Ipsum	Main Research Question	Q2	PM - Ben	Concept Testing	Medium
Lorem Ipsum	Main Research Question	Q3	Primary Contact	Usability Study	High
Payment	Fears and Concerns when using different payment methods	Q4	Design - Sam	Foundational Study	Medium
Deprioritized (Below the Line)					
Lorem Ipsum	Main Research Question	Q1	Primary Contact	Lorem Ipsum	Medium
Lorem Ipsum	Main Research Question	Q2	Primary Contact	Lorem Ipsum	Low
Lorem Ipsum	Main Research Question	Q3	Primary Contact	Lorem Ipsum	Medium
Lorem Ipsum	Main Research Question	Q4	Primary Contact	Lorem Ipsum	High

List out projects on a timeline to help visualize which weeks are going to be busy with parallel projects running and also provide a better sense of your upcoming schedule.

PLANNING
INFOGRAPHIC

| JAN | FEB | MAR | APR | MAY | JUN | JUL | AUG | SEP | OCT | NOV | DEC |

Lorem ipsum
Project A

Lorem ipsum
Project B

Lorem ipsum
Project C

Lorem ipsum
Project D

Lorem ipsum
Project E

Lorem ipsum
Project F

Lorem ipsum
Project G

Once the roadmap is finalized, get alignment and socialize. In this stage, sharing detailed information about all projects is highly effective and aids in obtaining buy-in from cross-functional partners ahead of time. It's recommended to disseminate the roadmap to all relevant stakeholders, including product partners, research teams, marketing teams, and products that intersect with the current project. Allow everyone to provide input at the initial stage, and then maintain continuous communication on the progress. Consistently distribute draft versions of the roadmap and then publish the final version once it has been solidified.

Following the above steps of drafting a roadmap with all possible projects, prioritizing based on resourcing and team priorities, and continuously socializing the plan can result in less thrash and stronger alignment with cross-functional partners.

However, do anticipate changes. Changes to the product roadmap frequently occur because of shifting business priorities that necessitate cross-functional partners to request ad hoc or modified research. *It's crucial to anticipate, embrace, and adapt to these changes.* While mapping out a six-month plan, it's advisable to specify details for only 6–12 weeks and then reevaluate progress at three-week intervals, making any necessary revisions or specifications mid-cycle.

KYLE BRADY, SR. UX RESEARCHER, INSTACART

A research roadmap—established at the beginning of each quarter or half—is one of the best tools you have as a user researcher. When done correctly, roadmapping sets you up for impact, improves prioritization, and helps lead the direction of the product. Done incorrectly, you will start projects just to stop them halfway through, uncover insights that won't be used, and generally be at the mercy of your partners when it comes to prioritization.

Truth be told, I didn't start formally roadmapping until about five years into my career as a user researcher. Before then, I didn't see myself as a strategic partner with my stakeholders. I would wait for a stakeholder to bring me a problem, then work with them to determine the appropriate research questions, the method I'd use, and the rest of the project parameters, all ad hoc. Not only was this process haphazard and stressful, but it felt like I was in the passenger seat of my own car—letting someone else drive my research and control my impact.

Enter roadmapping. Each half, I started putting together a detailed plan on how I would spend my time. Based on the strategy my product partners put together, I drafted a set of research questions, prioritized based on my assessment of the most pressing and important projects, and aligned with my stakeholders before the start of the half. This process was a step up from no roadmapping at all. From needing to constantly adjust my roadmap to support projects I probably should have planned for in the first place, roadmapping felt like a heroic, solo effort. It didn't result in the impact I had hoped for, and I still felt like I was in the passenger seat.

I still hadn't cracked the code.

Fast forward to the most obvious breakthrough of all time: I realized I had involved my stakeholders too late in the process. In the next half, I made it a point to start involving my stakeholders early and often in roadmapping.

- I started using brainstorming sessions. This helped to generate much more insightful questions due to both the diverse perspectives from the whole product team and the collective intelligence the team had about the product and the problem space.
- Based on the output of the brainstorms, I developed our high-level research questions and completed secondary research to determine if those questions had already been answered. This helped develop trust with my stakeholders—by showing both due diligence and want for efficiency—and made prioritization much easier.

- Finally, I worked with my primary stakeholders to prioritize the research questions for the half, which was a light lift, as they had been involved every step of the way.

This roadmapping process has put me in the driver's seat. More importantly, the process has made sure my stakeholders and I are always on the same page, which has led to greater impact, less thrash, and much more fulfilling and exciting work.

Utilize Creative Approaches for Sharing Research Findings

Simple presentations often do not cut it.

There are times when conventional presentations fall short, and we need to get creative with our formats. Simply conveying information is often insufficient, and instead, it's crucial to spark excitement and use captivating methods of presentation. As a presenter, I have experimented with various techniques that have been successful, and as an audience member, I have also witnessed compelling presentations that have been highly engaging.

Design Posters for Visual Storytelling

Transforming a deck of insights into a single-page format, such as a poster, can be a highly effective and powerful method for communicating research findings to stakeholders. This approach distills the information into a more digestible format, highlighting key insights and presenting them in a visually striking manner with the ability to incorporate graphics, images, and other design elements.

The poster can be conveniently appended to an email for easy consumption, allowing stakeholders to quickly and conveniently view the insights. Additionally, placing the posters in high-traffic areas of the workplace, such as conference rooms or common areas, can increase the visibility of the research findings, serving as a constant reminder to team members.

Moreover, these posters can serve as a point of reference for ongoing discussions or planning, as they provide a consolidated view of the research. This can be particularly helpful for cross-functional teams, allowing them to stay aligned and informed on key insights and priorities.

Organize Mini-Museums

The concept of a mini-museum involves visually displaying research findings in a large space and leveraging storytelling through artifacts.

You not only display insights on walls but also accompany them with pictures of participants and where they live, adding cultural nuances (when appropriate) or any other metadata that adds value. Mini-museums are effective when you have multiple studies around the same topic, and you can weave them all in and present them in a story format. After the content has been put on display, you invite stakeholders at a set time, and the researcher acts like a guide to the museum, sharing interesting facts and answering any questions the audience may have while taking them on this journey.

Host Trivia Day

Designing a game that incorporates research and data insights as questions can be an engaging and enjoyable way to educate and involve the audience. You can create a fun and interactive atmosphere while also imparting important knowledge. This approach can also help build teamwork and collaboration among team members.

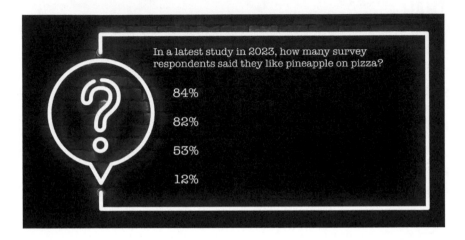

There are numerous ways to create such a game, but my most successful experience involved hosting it during a three-day team summit.

To execute this game, I set aside 1.5 hours when the entire team was together and divided them into smaller groups. The objective was straightforward: Each team was presented with multiple rounds of data and research questions in a multiple-choice format. Correct answers earned points for the team.

One of the most exciting rounds involved sharing new insights. I modified this round to resemble an open-book exam, sharing key findings on the spot and then asking questions related to them in the subsequent round. This tactic proved effective in encouraging cross-functional partners to pay attention and retain insights.

Enliven Presentations With Memes

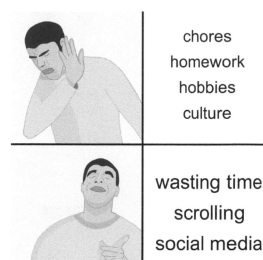

Using topic-relevant memes in a presentation can add a touch of color, personality, and humor to an otherwise dull presentation. In my experience, memes are particularly useful when transitioning to a new section of the presentation. They can effectively set the context for the upcoming slides and evoke a laugh from the audience, creating a more relaxed atmosphere.

However, it's important to use caution when incorporating memes into a presentation. You should avoid using them if presenting on an emotionally sensitive topic where laughter could be deemed inappropriate. Additionally, be mindful of the content of the memes you use, ensuring that they are not offensive or derogatory toward any particular group.

Create Artifacts

Certain research insights are relevant to short-term projects, while others serve as guiding principles for the team over the course of several years. But how do you remind yourself and others of those insights time and again without being continuously in presentation mode?

One effective way that I have witnessed that ensures that your research insights have a lasting impact is to print them as artifacts. By doing so, you create a physical object that people can keep close, refer to often, and share with others. This approach is especially useful if your research has insights that are going to be relevant and valuable for a long time. Do make sure that your artifact is clear, well-designed, accessible, and distributed widely to maximize its impact.

One of my co-researchers came up with a brilliant way to do this. He had been working on measuring product success metrics, and he wanted to make sure that everyone on the team was aware of them. So, he printed them out in the same size and format as our office badges and asked team members to place them alongside their badges.

Like me, you might think it was just a piece of paper, right? Yes, a piece of paper but with mighty potential. Since then, every time I looked at my badge, I was reminded of the product success criteria, and if there was a discussion in the room, the badge gave us a little nudge, a gentle reminder of what we were working toward. It was as if the badges had become talismans, little reminders of what we were striving for. The impact of this simple idea was incredible. It kept us focused and motivated, and it helped us keep the end goal in sight.

Generate Empathy by Using Team Members as Research Participants

Research is a powerful tool for discovering pain points that users encounter while interacting with a product or service. These pain points can be as simple as a tedious sign-up page or a checkout process that requires extensive calculations to maximize discounts. As researchers, it's our responsibility to not only identify these pain points but also find solutions to alleviate them.

One strategy that I have found to be effective is that before sharing the research insight, I pause and ask my cross-functional partners to try the activity themselves, such as trying signing up or checking out themselves. This approach is similar to replicating the study, but instead of users, our team members act as participants.

When cross-functional partners experience these pain points firsthand, they register much more effectively, and they're more likely to be motivated to find effective solutions. This also ensures that everyone has a shared understanding of the user's perspective, helps align the team around common goals, and can lead to more effective solutions that cater to the user's needs.

You might be wondering why these are occasional strategies and not suitable for everyday use because when overdone, they lose their desirability and uniqueness.

Acknowledgments

I am immensely grateful to the wonderful people in my life who have been a part of this incredible journey and supported me in writing this book. Let's be real—without these people, this book would probably just be a bunch of incoherent ramblings and doodles.

I would like to express my gratitude . . . To my amazing parents, who are my pillars of strength. Your unwavering support and belief in me have made me the person I am today. Thank you for being my guiding light and my biggest cheerleader. Without your love and encouragement, I would not have been able to pursue my dreams and complete this book.

To my loving husband, Ashish, who has been my confidant, my rock, and my constant support system. Thank you for always being there for me, cheering me on, and pushing me to achieve my goals. From the smallest triumphs to the toughest challenges, you have stood by my side, offering guidance, encouragement, and unconditional love. Thank you for being my strength and for everything you do.

To my dear brother, Nihit, who is an eternal student of life and an endless source of inspiration. I am grateful for your encouragement and boundless support. And, of course, for being a good sport despite knowing deep down that mom loves me more. To my sister-in-law, Mayuri, your kind words and enthusiasm have always made a positive impact on my life.

To my father-in-law, who may have nagged me a bit to finish this book, but without whose constant push, this book would never be complete. Your feedback has been invaluable in shaping it and getting it done. To my mother-in-law, who has been a constant source of support and encouragement and has always believed in me. Thank you for always having my back and keeping my kids alive (and clean) so I could focus on writing.

To my sister-in-law, Krista, who was the first to read my book and gave me the encouragement I needed to keep going. Love you for laughing at all my unfunny jokes, lovingly supporting me, and being there unconditionally. To my brother-in-law, Tushar, the visionary entrepreneur who's working hard to create a legacy, so I can afford to write without worrying about the bills. Thank you for inspiring us to pursue our passions fearlessly.

To my beautiful kids, Adya and Vedika, who fill my life with joy, laughter, and endless love, you are my reason to keep going. I thank you for inspiring me every single day (and enlightening me that sometimes it's okay to eat ice cream for breakfast).

To my wonderful nieces and nephew, Kavya, Adamya, Anisha, and Yashi, who complete my life and bring endless happiness and warmth to it. Thank you for your love and for being an important part of my journey.

To Isabel Martin, whose creative genius and artistic vision breathed life into the captivating book cover. Your meticulous attention to detail and ability to encapsulate the essence of my work visually is truly commendable.

To my amazing contributors, some of the most brilliant people I know, whose love, dedication, and hard work have made this book a reality and to whom I owe many drinks. Kam, Amelie, Linnea, Anne, Aditya, Anubhav, Lillian, Kyle, Theo, Sean, Ilana, Sarah, Wyatt, Tom, Kevin, Omer, Saeideh, Todd, Ali, and Stephanie, I thank you all from the bottom of my heart for making this book infinitely better and putting up with my countless edits and rewrites.

To Randi and Solomon from Taylor and Francis for their exceptional enthusiasm and dedication throughout this journey. Their belief in the importance of this project, coupled with their continuous availability to offer guidance, brainstorm ideas, and provide unwavering assistance, has been a driving force behind the successful completion of this endeavor. My gratitude also extends to Jayachandran R and reviewers and editors from Apex CoVantage, who diligently oversaw the preparation of my book for publishing. Your expertise in managing the intricate processes involved in bringing this book to print has been indispensable, and I am thankful for all your support.

To my beloved mentors, Tim Loving, Rebecca Destello, Mike Yaklin, Dan Kutz, and countless others, who have been my compass and sounding board. I am deeply grateful for your endless inspiration, never-ending support, and tireless encouragement that has guided me on this journey.

To my designer, Junaid Khan, who created different designs and images for the book. Thank you for your promptness and willingness to make so many revisions.

Last but not least, to my dearest Nimisha Di, Aayushie, and Nonie, my in-house legal experts, who provided valuable advice and expertise that was a source of comfort.

Thank you all from the bottom of my heart. I am incredibly fortunate to have such an exceptional support system.

Index